STUDIES IN
VICTORIAN LITERATURE

BY

STANLEY T. WILLIAMS

NEW YORK
E. P. DUTTON & COMPANY
681 FIFTH AVENUE

Col. 2ᵃ

Euglir · H. 0 C .

TO

M. L. W.

Foreword

THE criticism of Victorian literature goes on apace. Hardly a month passes which does not give to the world the biography or the journal or the reminiscences of some distinguished Victorian. This group of essays does not aim to subvert established judgments or to determine, in such criticism, new principles. I have written them, at intervals during a period of four years, as an expression of the belief that one may learn much concerning an age by haunting its bypaths. Some of the books considered are not of the first rank (Charles Kingsley's *Yeast* and George Brimley's *Essays,* for example, are nearly forgotten) ; and some of the great thinkers studied here are regarded from particular points of view. (Who thinks often of Cardinal Newman as a critic of literature? Or of Clough's prose?) But such an approach to literature creates intimacies which have distinction and also a unique advantage: they make us revaluate. One may press boldly into the throng, or one may watch carefully, somewhat apart, the familiar pageant; and so detect perhaps the old faces illumined by a different light, or hear in the old voices new tones. In the criticism of literature something may be said for the art of overhearing. In this way indeed unexpected values may be established.

Thus it is my conviction that, disparate as they are, each book or person here thought worthy of an essay projects a tendency of the Victorian era. This is the thread which binds together these essays.

Foreword

Both Thomas Carlyle and Matthew Arnold were wont to speak of the many and confused voices of the nineteenth century. My essays are, I hope, true echoes of those voices,—echoes which may help to clarify the confusion. Possibly they may add something to our understanding of the Victorian age, an age whose history is still unwritten.

Some of the essays, often in quite different form, have appeared in periodicals. For permission to reprint these I wish to thank the editors of the *North American Review;* the *Literary Review;* the *Sewanee Review;* the *South Atlantic Quarterly;* the *University of California Chronicle;* the *Texas Review;* and the *English Journal.* I am especially indebted, for assistance in the revision of this manuscript, to Professor Henry A. Beers.

S.T.W.

Yale University
 March 3, 1923.

Contents

Carlyle's "Life of John Sterling"

Carlyle's "Life of John Sterling"

An excellent way to begin a study of Victorian literature is to read Carlyle's *Life of John Sterling*. It is even possible that this book is the best approach to Carlyle himself; but this is debatable. There can, however, be little doubt that an attempt to understand John Sterling's experience enriches our comprehension of the age. We sense the strength of those cross-currents of thought, which, after all—in spite of Carlyle's reiterations that Sterling mastered them and was a radiant child of the empyrean—left this gifted protégé of Carlyle's intellectually confused. Sterling was a puzzled spirit. In politics he tried to be a radical and failed. In literature he was unsuccessful. As for the Church, it may be said that he would, but dared not; he dared, but could not. Carlyle says that Sterling wished merely to live a noble life. This, one feels, he could not help doing; to this he was born by nature. But the outward expression of his idealism was erratic. He wandered from one profession to another, from doubt to conviction, and again to doubt. This was partly temperament; Sterling was volatile. But it was chiefly bewilderment in an epoch of conflicting opinions. Sterling could not make up his mind about things.

If, through Carlyle's book, we live over again Sterling's life, we feel keenly the doubts which assailed him. We see him encounter men of all faiths: the utilitarian, the Unitarian, and the Angli-

3

can; and we react with him to thinkers so different as Julius Hare, Coleridge, and Carlyle himself. And through his suggestion we visualize other great leaders in nineteenth-century thought. The book is a beryl-stone in which we see prophets both of the past and of the present. In this biography, although not all these are mentioned by Carlyle, we seem to find all the ferment of conflicting faiths. Newman is at Littlemore, and shop-window posters bear index fingers pointing towards Rome. Carlyle describes Christianity as "Hebrew Old-clothes." At the hest of his dearest master, Maurice, Charles Kingsley is preaching the doctrines of the *Kingdom of Christ*. Matthew Arnold declares that Newman's solution "to speak frankly, is impossible"; and against it places his resigned faith in a "Not-ourselves which makes for righteousness." Meanwhile, Clough at Oxford, certainly the spokesman for many young Englishmen of his day, alludes to himself as "drawn up like a straw by the draught of a chimney." Many of these phenomena of belief appear after Sterling's time, but their origins are in Carlyle's book, and all of them are visible during a few decades about the middle of the century. "Yeast!" Kingsley called them. To these vagaries of thought no one was more sensitive than Carlyle. Of the voices which haunted the memory of Matthew Arnold long afterwards, one was Carlyle's, then, he says, still puissant, and not yet over-strained. Never was that voice less strained than in the *Life of John Sterling*. Carlyle denounces, of course, but there is no bitterness in the book—rather sweetness of spirit. And in its pages is reflected the England of the first half of the century, the England that Henry Adams understood, the England of embattled beliefs.

The serenity of tone in the *Life of John Sterling,* so unusual in Carlyle, proceeds from his affection for Sterling. The proofs of Carlyle's unfailing sympathy with human beings are innumerable. A contemporary writer has described the infinite pity written on Carlyle's face. The anecdote of the shoes in the essay on Samuel Johnson or of the tanneries of Meudon in the *French Revolution* are but two of the myriad incidents in Carlyle's writings, all so different, yet all arising at the same source, his compassion. In the *Life of John Sterling* this feeling is accentuated, personal. Carlyle's voice is unstrained because he speaks of one whom he loves. Upon this mood the influence of the book is somewhat dependent; for this reason we are apt to turn to it again. But the persuasive power of the biography, as a record of the past, is bound up also with the truthfulness of what Carlyle says of Sterling. The reader may check the facts for himself either in Archdeacon Hare's account of Sterling, or elsewhere, in, for example, Caroline Fox's *Memories of Old Friends.* If we make allowance for Carlyle's own interpretation of events, as in his explanation for Sterling's short stay in the Anglican fold, we confront, not a romantic figure, but a man whose intellectual experience was precisely what Carlyle depicts it to have been: an unsuccessful search for truth.

5

That Sterling was a real man is important. There are other books which reflect the speculative thought of the nineteenth century, and these are helpful primers for the novice, but such are either truthful records, unheightened by great literary power, like Caroline Fox's book, or, like Kingsley's novel, *Yeast,* they are fiction. The power of the *Life of John Sterling* resides in the fact that it is neither uninspired, nor fictitious. It is the story of a real man, truthfully related by a person of genius.

Another reason for meeting the Victorians first through the *Life of John Sterling* is that the book admits the reader at once to intimacy with *literati* to whom he has been properly but distantly presented through their dignified and, sometimes, boring books. I have a friend who insists upon knowing authors before he reads their books. He must chat with Mr. Masefield ere he will read a line of him; he will not see *Loyalties* until some club corner has yielded up Mr. Galsworthy. Such an ideal invites disillusionment, but it may be realized mildly by reading the *Life of John Sterling.* We dine with Carlyle's friends or walk London town with them. Years may elapse before we read the theological writings of Frederick Denison Maurice, but if we see him with Sterling in the *Athenæum* adventure, or at Sterling's death-bed, we are likely to think of him justly, and with some admiration. It is interesting, too, to see Sterling and John Stuart Mill together in the Sistine Chapel. We meet also, in one of Carlyle's sketches, "Good little Frank" Edgeworth,

Carlyle's "Life of John Sterling"

> "a short neat man; of sleek, square, colourless face (resembling the Portraits of his Father), with small blue eyes in which twinkled curiously a joyless smile; his voice was croaky and shrill, with a touch of shrewish obstinacy in it, and perhaps of sarcasm withal. A composed, dogmatic, speculative, exact, and not melodious man."

Here, too, is Francis Newman,

> "then and still an ardently inquiring soul, of fine University and other attainments, of sharp-cutting restlessly advancing intellect, and the mildest pious enthusiasm."

There are glimpses of others: Richard Trench, then far from *Words* and the Archbishopric of Dublin; Jacky Kemble; Baconian Spedding; Apollo-like George Venables, destined to break Thackeray's nose, and to become George Warrington in *Pendennis;* Keatsian Milnes, too. Truly, we have broken Victorian privacy. Seldom has Carlyle's hand limned more vividly than in this book.

A considerable portion of the biography is concerned with Sterling's prose and poetry. The works of Sterling some have talked of, but few have read. Carlyle cannot persuade us to take Sterling seriously as a man of letters. Indeed, he scarcely tries. Sterling's books are found on remote shelves of large libraries. Alphabetically, chronologically, or in order of merit, the seasoned reader consumes them late in life. There is pleasure in dipping into them, for they are the expression of a winning personality. But no more: through Carlyle and through Carlyle alone shall we remember Sterling. In the *Onyx*

7

Ring, which *Blackwood's* brought out in 1838, Carlyle himself is a protagonist. Edmonston, the hero, passing weary of his own personality, assumes, by means of a magic ring, those of his friends. Archdeacon Hare, under a fragile disguise, is his first new identity. Dull satiety creeps in; he no longer cares to be even Archdeacon Hare. Another personality, that of a hermit, is clearly an adumbration of Carlyle. This person denounces political parties; he decries happiness; he is described as the most marked and original figure in modern England. Nevertheless, Edmonston makes finally a decision frequently arrived at in life: it is more interesting to work out one's own disagreeable destiny than the pleasanter fates of friends. He puts his old cloak about him; Edmonston becomes Edmonston and marries his first love.

Arthur Coningsby, the youthful novel of 1833, and the *Essays and Tales,* published by Parker in 1848, are still less convincing. To accept any judgment of Carlyle's concerning poetry, even Sterling's, is surprising. His assertion that Shakespeare should have stuck to prose has persuaded some that Carlyle never left childhood æsthetically. The remark, however, was merely petulant. Carlyle is sometimes a good critic of poetry. His criticisms of Sterling's verse are just. Of *Strafford,* the tragedy dedicated to Emerson, Carlyle writes:

"Before going to Italy he had sent me the Manuscript; . . . willing to hear the worst that could be said of his

poetic enterprise. I had to afflict him again, the good
brave soul, with the deliberate report that I could *not*
accept this Drama as his Picture of the Life of Strafford,
or as any *Picture* of that strange Fact."

Yet there are in *Strafford* noble passages.

The Election, too, Sterling's comic poem, is read-
able. *The Sexton's Daughter,* however, is a rare bit
of fustian. The poem is Wordsworthian and affords
ample proof that the founder of the Lake School
was, for the Victorians certainly, inimitable. Its
story is of Henry, the school-teacher, in love with the
daughter of the Sexton. This tyrant, true to the
traditions of cruel fathers, tries to lure Henry into
the profession of grave-digging. He has the pardonable illusion that grave-digging is more lucrative than
teaching. In his criticism Carlyle bolsters up the
poem with rather noisy rhetoric. It is said, however,
that when he finished reading the poem for the first
time he snarled: "Goody-goody!" Poor Sterling!
He failed in literature, as in so many other ventures.

Sterling's failures are bound up in the great problem of his life, his attitude towards the Church, an
attitude which takes us back always to a single man,
Coleridge. Sterling had been deeply influenced by
Coleridge's faith in the Anglican Church. In considering the relation of Coleridge to Sterling, Carlyle
draws his superb portrait of Coleridge at Highgate,
a portrait which reduces the vignettes we have been
discussing to the position, by contrast, of thumb-nail
sketches. Carlyle reveals clearly the truth about
Coleridge: that he was in many ways in Victorian

thought a first cause. Its woof is woven of the threads of his philosophy. At one time, it has been justly remarked, all young Englishmen were thinking in terms of Coleridge. His mind was above all else seminal, and growths from his thought were everywhere. "Coleridge moonshine" was an intellectual fashion. Such a turn of thought as the Broad Church Movement owed its existence in large measure to Coleridge's *Aids to Reflection*.

But Coleridge affected his contemporaries less by writing than by speech. To know him one must turn from his unfinished books to the records of his conversation—those strange fantasies of obscurity and wisdom. *Viva voce* portraits of him are numerous, and all such are precious. Among others is Emerson's sketch. He describes Coleridge's regret that Doctor Channing had been a Unitarian. It was, he said, an unspeakable misfortune. The metaphysician then read furiously from a book execrating all Unitarians. But Emerson interrupted mildly: "I was born and bred a Unitarian." "Yes, I supposed so," replied the other and redoubled his anathemas. Many other portraits of Coleridge survive, from the hands of Scott, Southey, Hazlitt, De Quincey, and Wordsworth. As we think of Carlyle's picture of him at the end of his life, it is well, perhaps, to recall the famous apostrophe of Lamb, depicting him in youth.

"Come back into memory . . ." Lamb cries, "Samuel Taylor Coleridge—Logician, Metaphysician, Bard!— How have I seen the casual passer through the Cloisters stand still, entranced with admiration, . . . to hear thee unfold, in thy deep and sweet intonations, the mysteries of Jamblichus, or Plotinus (for even in those years thou waxedst not pale at such philosophic draughts), or reciting Homer in his Greek, or Pindar— while the walls of the old Grey Friars reechoed to the accents of the *inspired charity-boy!*"

Yet of all portraits Carlyle's is the most personal, the most suggestive, easily the greatest in literature. This chapter alone makes the *Life of John Sterling* an admirable portal to Victorian literature. Sir George Trevelyan, speaking of the literary conservatism of his uncle in his *Life and Letters of Lord Macaulay*, says:

"Little as he was aware of it, it was no slight privation that one . . . who so keenly relished the exquisite trifling of Plato should never have tasted the description of Coleridge's talk in the *Life of John Sterling.*"

That the real Coleridge looks out from Carlyle's picture is apparent from Coleridge's own memorials of his life. A letter to Mr. Poole, written in 1797, depicting his dreamy boyhood, is like the opening scene of the drama whose final act Carlyle describes:

"Coleridge," Carlyle writes, "sat on the brow of Highgate Hill, in those years, looking down on London and its smoke-tumult, like a sage escaped from the inanity of life's battle; attracting towards him the thoughts of innumerable brave souls engaged there . . . He had, especially among young inquiring men, a higher than literary, a kind of prophetic or magician character . . . A sublime man who, alone in those dark days had saved his crown of spiritual manhood."

"Coleridge moonshine," Carlyle thought, unsettled Sterling and other young Englishmen in their attitude towards the Church. They had a healthy intolerance of its shibboleths, but the mage was forever exhorting them: *"Esto perpetua!"* Sterling wavered. On the threshold he shrank from the "black dragoon in every parish, on good pay and rations, horse meat and man's meat." The "black dragoon" was the smug country parson, equipped with pony carriage for wife and children, who buried himself in the trivia of theological controversy. This lie Sterling would not live. His was the odd quest, not of orthodoxy, but of Truth. Instead of entering the Church he played restlessly with original and even dangerous turns of thought. With Carlyle he drank deeply of speculative German philosophy. He never became what Hare made him out, "a pale sickly shadow in torn surplice," for he loved what belonged to manhood, and he possessed the intellectual and moral courage to face doubt.

But despite this Sterling did at last a characteristic thing of the age: he took orders. He did this under the discipline of events grave and saddening. Carlyle emphasizes the fact that this was a false step, but it was a very natural and not unbeautiful thing that Sterling in the time of his distress returned to the faith of his fathers. When they are at their wits' end they call upon Him. Sterling, however, remained in the fold exactly eight months. Was ill health, as given out, the reason for his defection? Carlyle will not believe it. Unquestionably, the taking of orders was an aberration. The real Sterling could never be a churchman. He was rather the representative of his generation, both in the uncertainty of his faith, and in his final repudiation of the English Church. Sterling left the Church with his belief in Christianity shattered; his love for it remained the same. Carlyle makes Sterling's experience vivid; he also leaves no doubt that this tragedy was enacted daily. His whole book protests that the Church of England of that day could not satisfy the needs of thoughtful young men.

From Sterling's dissatisfaction with the Church we learn much. His perception that its formulas were outworn prepares us for later upheavals, and explains the weakness of the Church in its battles against dissension within and attacks from without. The black dragoon was but a feeble antagonist against a Newman or a Darwin. More than this, Sterling's experience throws light on the problem of Carlyle's own religion. That inarticulate faith of his should be studied with the aid of every incident, fact, or comment that we can marshal from Carlyle's writings. Froude's exposition is none too clear or complete, and offhand remarks of Carlyle's add to the confusion. There are the sneers at the "Hebrew Old-clothes" of Christianity; the reported declaration that it was as sure as mathematics that such things as the Christian miracles never happened. And these statements are coupled with the puzzling assurance which Carlyle gave his mother that basically his belief and hers concerning God were identical.

13

What are we to make of all this? The only possible answer is that we must try to reconcile for ourselves seemingly contradictory beliefs, and construct, if we can, a consistent summary of Carlyle's opinions on religion. For this the *Life of John Sterling* is useful. Although Carlyle himself refers to it as "a poor tatter of a thing," the book is, nevertheless, filled with pregnant reflections on Sterling's spiritual history, and thus furnishes supplemental evidence for a final estimate of Carlyle's religion.

Sometimes, indeed, this biography seems merely a medium for Carlyle's own opinions. The reader is never allowed to forget who is speaking; one Thomas Carlyle, prophet of the nineteenth century. He resembles an orchestra leader attempting a difficult symphony. And occasionally he seems to leap upon the stage, baton in hand! All these judgments concerning Sterling have a strong Carlylean bias. Thus Carlyle's dislike of his friend's "japannish" classicality was born of his own distaste for the classics. Among the Greeks he himself cared only for Homer. Far better, he asserted, was the bold Scandinavian mythology. Here, in the *Life of John Sterling,* we may behold the whimsical preferences of "the Goth of literature," with his aversion to Keats and Byron; his dislike of Horace; and his admiration for such antitheses as Sterne and Richter.

It is as if Carlyle's personality had cast over Sterling's life a gigantic shadow, thus rendering the book unique among biographies. Sterling is dwarfed by a kindred but mightier spirit. One feels an unequal marriage of true minds. Sterling is present, but chiefly because he is seen by "those devouring eyes; those thirsty eyes; those portrait-eating, portrait-painting eyes," as Emerson described Carlyle's power of visualization. After all is said, the most extraordinary aspect of the *Life of John Sterling* is that, in concluding it, one thinks not of the biographee but of the biographer. Boswell, Hallam Tennyson, William Michael Rossetti are lost in the hierophants they worship, but in this book the process is reversed: John Sterling is swallowed up in Thomas Carlyle. Everyone knows the biographies of men of genius written by men of talent. The *Life of John Sterling* is a biography of a man of talent written by a man of genius.

This genius will make us remember Sterling. Because of Carlyle the student of Victorian literature understands better the fightings and despondings of certain Victorians.

> "Here, visible to myself, for some while, was a brilliant human presence, distinguishable, honourable and lovable amid the dim common populations; among the million little beautiful, once more a beautiful human soul: whom I, among others, recognized and lovingly walked with, while the years and hours were."

Sterling's gift for friendships was prodigious, and has helped him to put on, to some extent, immortality. He was capable of a lasting intimacy with a man three thousand miles away whom he had never seen. Carlyle introduced Sterling to Emerson by letter; their correspondence proves the warmth of their friendship.

The vital friendship of Sterling's life was with Carlyle himself. Just after the appearance in *Fraser's* of that shocking parable, *Sartor Resartus,* with its Teutonic syntax and its snow-rose-bloom-maidens, Mill brought the two together. Sterling's subsequent review of *Sartor* recommended it to many bewildered readers, and gave it fame among Carlyle's contemporaries. The secret of this friendship, which persisted until Sterling's death, may be guessed. Sterling was not a "hero." But Carlyle found in their attitudes towards life a basic agreement, and the stimulus, too, of something else. Our best friends are those who understand us, but who supply, also, a spiritual need. What struck Carlyle with wonder was Sterling's optimism. As the friendship deepened, this became a complement of his own sad nature. For Carlyle, though he spoke much of hope, was seldom hopeful. And Sterling cheered him.

This sunniness was, indeed, Sterling's glory. To poverty, to disease, to the spiritual maladies of the age—and to such he was keenly susceptible—he opposed a rare courage. Besieged by trouble, he writes Emerson:

> "But after all regrets, Life is good—to see the face of Truth, and enjoy the beauty of tears and smiles, and know one's self a man, and love what belongs to manhood, all this is a blessing that may console us for all wants, and *that* sickness and sorrow, and, one may trust, Death, cannot take away."

Death approached, but on the verge Sterling sent a brave word to America: "I fear nothing," he wrote to Emerson, "and hope much." At the very last he wrote this letter, a strangely beautiful memorial of his affection for Carlyle:

"My Dear Carlyle,—For the first time for many months it seems possible to send you a few words; merely, however, for Remembrance and Farewell. On higher matters there is nothing to say. I tread the common road into the great darkness, without any thought of fear, and with very much of hope. Certainty indeed I have none. With regard to You and Me I cannot begin to write; having nothing for it but to keep shut the lid of those secrets with all the iron weights that are in my power. Towards me it is still more true than towards England that no man has been and done like you. Heaven bless you! If I can lend a hand when THERE, that will not be wanting. It is all very strange, but not one hundredth part so sad as it seems to the standers-by. . . .

JOHN STERLING."

Carlyle's "Past and Present": A Prophecy

Carlyle's "Past and Present": A Prophecy

ONE day when Mr. Arthur Henderson was stating in no uncertain terms what would be acceptable to the British Labour Party, a member of the audience was moved to quote to his neighbour a sentence from Carlyle's *Past and Present:* "Some 'Chivalry of Labour,' some noble Humanity and practical Divineness of labour, will yet be realized on this Earth." With its growth, then, the Labour Party had become "chivalrous," if not divine; the speaker's tone was that of complacence, of realized prophecy. "Chivalrous" and "divine" are not the adjectives we all apply readily to the Labour Party, but everyone would admit the fitness of one epithet: powerful. Every history of industrialism, socialism, or political development proclaims the enlargement of the Labour Party. During the eighty years since the appearance of *Past and Present* (1843) it has advanced whip and spur; so much so that much of Carlyle's radicalism seems now curiously antiquated. For this very reason it was surprising to hear *Past and Present* quoted so appositely. A book good enough in its day, we fancied: but is it not now obsolete?

Apparently, not wholly so. Social thinkers still refer to it. They do so chiefly because of the last section of the book. It will be remembered that this is called *Horoscope,* and that it is a passionate, if somewhat incoherent, visualization of the future of labour in the light of the past, and of the England of 1843. Lovers of Carlyle recollect more distinctly the chapters on Abbot Samson and the life at Bury St. Edmund. On the other hand, students interested in the records of social progress turn to *Horoscope*. This chapter they may find amusing in various ways, but they also think it suggestive, even prophetic. *Past and Present* deals as much with the unknown future as with the known past. Carlyle dogmatizes on the twelfth century; he speculates concerning the twentieth.

Many critics have been inclined to discount Carlyle's speculations about the future because, they say, he had no really constructive philosophy for the present. How often they tell us that as a critic of society he is merely destructive. "Destructive" and "constructive" are dangerous words when used as flat categories. The bitter dramatist, Ibsen, is, I understand, now that his flagellation of society has brought results, regarded as a constructive critic. In this sense Carlyle, too, perhaps, is constructive. But, aside from an examination of the real significance of the terms which we apply to Carlyle so glibly, something might be said for the position that even in his own day he was constructive. Too little is made of this possibility. Emerson remarked that the question of humanity alone really interested Carlyle. Had he then nothing definite to propose, except, as we are asked to believe, a chimera of hero-worship? Is he simply an apostle of the ethical philosophers, saying: "Make thyself a man better to be governed"? "Reform thyself"? This is, of course, the core of his remedy. But a reasonably coherent body of what men call practical reform may be put together from the writings of Carlyle.

He urged, for instance, that the Crown appoint the ten most capable men in Parliament to govern England. And his recommendations concerning the great questions of Emigration and Education were sensible. The confusion about Carlyle's destructive criticism comes from an imperfect understanding of the conflict in his mind between his hopes for democracy and his belief in sovereignty. He insists on sovereignty, and we can trace the waning of his faith in democracy as he becomes gradually convinced that democracy will not achieve proper sovereignty. He realizes that democracy is inevitable, but thinks it incompatible with what he believes to be true sovereignty. Since he never relinquished the idea that sovereignty was indispensable, we find him at last striving to arrive at some solution by which democracy and sovereignty may be reconciled. And his scheme for attaining this end is surely not without some constructive value. What must be done, he says, is to bring together more closely the class which represents sovereignty in England and the class which represents democracy. That is, both the so-called upper and the lower classes must be trained to recognize true sovereignty. All men must be permeated with a clearer notion of what true leadership is. The means to achieve this realization are two: Emigration and Education. England is overpopulated. Those who from poverty are hopelessly be-

yond uplift should try their fortunes elsewhere. For
the rest education should labour. This is not all,
but it is enough to indicate that all Carlyle's talk
is not, as many would have us think, a babble
of "eternal immensities" and metaphysical "flame-
images."

A reconsideration of *Past and Present* has interest, then, for two reasons. First, for its own
sake, because it helps us to understand more distinctly Carlyle's attitude towards the "condition of
England question," and thus aids us in qualifying
the popular truisms about his philosophy, and,
second, because its prophecies make it unusual among
Carlyle's writings. *Horoscope* enables us to see our
own social problems in clearer perspective. For the
first, it is well to remind ourselves how acute a
criticism *Past and Present* is upon the England of
eighty years ago. Although hastily written, it was,
nevertheless, enriched by Carlyle's deepest wisdom
and ennobled by his most eloquent manner. Mr.
John Morley, re-reading it in 1891, exclaimed:
"What energy, what inexhaustible vigour, what incomparable humour, what substantial justice of insight, and what sublimity of phrase and image." Of
these qualities in the book, and of its high originality
of design, much has already been written, but even
now, when its work is accomplished, we can glance
at it again with profit.

What impresses us now is what has impressed
every reader of the book since 1843: its overwhelming
fervour. A student of political history of the 'thirties

24

and 'forties once told me that the disorders of that
time never seemed real to him until he read *Past and
Present*. When Carlyle pushed across the table to
his wife the manuscript of the *French Revolution,*
he cried: "You have not had for a hundred years
any book that comes more direct and flamingly from
the heart of a living man." His comment might
have included *Past and Present*. Yet in spite of the
apparently careless enthusiasm of the book, Carlyle
used in its composition the method of the literary
artist.

Carlyle's technique always seems inherent in the
man himself. It is less conscious art than his way
of looking at things. His artistic methods are, if
we like, mannerisms. But conscious or unconscious,
the principles in this method are interesting. One
principle in *Past and Present* is Carlyle's repeated
use of personal, concrete detail. Over the analyst's
account of the Manchester insurrection we nod; over
Carlyle's, even today, we instinctively clench our
fists. For here "persons influence us, voices melt us,
looks subdue us, deeds inflame us." Manchester is
become, derisively, Peterloo. This riot is in Carlyle's
pages a series of stirring images: "Woolwich grape-
shot will sweep clear all the streets"; or, "there lie
poor sallow work-worn weavers, and complain no
more now." Many writers felt the anguish of these
poor people. Tennyson, in *Maud,* describes the
misery connected with "chalk and alum and plaster."
But Carlyle shocks us into an understanding of the
suffering of the 'forties by unforgettable anecdotes:

that, for instance, of the parents found guilty of poisoning three children, in order to defraud a burial society of £3 8s. due by law upon the death of each child. I have often wondered whether Carlyle and Tennyson, in their intimacy, had not talked over this incident, for we have Tennyson's line: "When a Mammonite mother kills her babe for a burial fee." This was a story likely to awaken even the British Philistine. After this resignation to human suffering seemed less easy. The device of personal detail may, of course, be found everywhere in Carlyle. We encounter it particularly in his relentless pictures of the French Revolution. But it is singularly well adapted for such a diatribe as *Past and Present*.

Such detail, however, is not always ghastly. To emphasize the talk of Parliament Carlyle says much of "oceans of horse-hair, continents of parchment"; to accentuate the sin of indifference he relates sardonically the history of that race near the Dead Sea: it "listened with real tedium to Moses, with light grinning, or with splenetic sniffs and sneers." Much of the detail is vivid, cheerful incident. But still more of it might be distinguished as imaginative allusion. As a reader Carlyle had despoiled all literature; he boasted that while at Craigenputtock he had read everything. *Past and Present* is a mosaic of allusion. Sometimes Carlyle caps a sentence with a phrase—such as the "Behemoth of Chaos"—and then does not employ it again. More often an illustration echoes through the book:

Carlyle's "Past and Present": A Prophecy

"The day's wages of John Milton's day's work, named
Paradise Lost and Milton's *Works,* were Ten Pounds,
paid by instalments, and a rather close escape from death
on the gallows."

An ingenious variation in the use of myths is to drive
home, by means of them, the idea of a chapter or of
a succession of chapters. Thus *Midas* and *The
Sphinx* are chapter captions; in each case Carlyle
applies, by implication, the parables to England. In
the first the "baleful fiat as of enchantment" prevents
the conversion of the nation's wealth into real pros-
perity; and in the second, England, since she has
failed to answer the riddle of life truly, is being torn
to pieces. It is impossible to exaggerate the mul-
tiplicity of Carlyle's analogies. There appear, one
after the other, in *Past and Present* personages from
history, gods from mythology, and figures from obscure corners of fiction. *Horoscope,* in particular,
is like a stream bearing along the *disjecta membra*
of literature and history. In this section, in juxtaposition hardly closer than that given them here, are:
Columbus, Thersites, Mahomet, Cromwell, Wallace,
Igdrasil, Byron, Pilate, King John, Hydra-Coil,
Jötuns, Rhadamanthus, Burns, the Iliad, Kilkenny
Cats, and Lakenheath eels! Such an inundation
stimulates at first, then fatigues. But the total effect
is that of eloquence and brilliance of manner.

Carlyle's allusions seem most pungent when they
are fictitious. He refers solemnly and without explanation to individuals whom he evidently regards
as already intimates of the reader. He never, for

example, introduces us formally to Plugson of Undershot. Who, pray, are Colacorde, Blusterowski, and Schnüspel? It is entertaining to know that "Schnüspel, the distinguished Novelist," is Charles Dickens. All Yankee-land hurrahs him on his lecture tour. But it is just as pleasant to realize that we cannot label other effigies so exactly, for instance, Colacorde and Blusterowski. Their flavour depends not upon who they are, but upon what they connote. Every aviary has birds whose ludicrousness is surpassed only by their absurd self-esteem. Someone has profanely said that God created the grotesque beasts and birds in a fit of laughter. Figures like Mr. Facing-both-Ways, Viscount Mealymouth, Earl of Windlestraw, or Diogenes Teufelsdröckh furnish the best proof that Carlyle had a sense of humour. As Charles Lamb loved a fool, so Carlyle delighted in a grotesque. Sir Jabesh Windbag is perfect, without analysis; so is Sauerteig of the *Houndsditch Indicator,* and Bobus Higgins, "sausage-maker on the great scale." "In the matter of elections," Carlyle remarks, "what can the incorruptiblest *Bobuses* elect, if it be not some Bobissimus?" No one would give up readily these Carlylean gargoyles.

Carlyle commandeers, indeed, every stylistic device which he knows, for his attacks in *Past and Present* on the strongholds of English apathy. The book has an amazing exuberance of expression. Nowhere is it more true, as one critic has remarked, that Carlyle seems to think and write with his whole body. Through four long parts of the book he

28

belabours his twenty-seven millions of English fools, the numbskulls of his generation. He pleads with them, exhorts them, satirizes them, reasons with them, and denounces them. His hyperbole is a little tiresome, but he convinces by his honesty, and he holds our interest by the profusion of illustration and anecdote. We can find violence without distinction in other pamphlets of the time. *Past and Present* is more effective than these, partly from these Carlylean mannerisms.

If the style of *Past and Present* is unique, the structure of the book is not less so. The underlying principle of Carlyle's lesson is a return to the past for precepts. One characteristic of a materialistic present is something more than a sense of superiority over the past, in respect to government, religion, and social conditions. We do not merely express indifference to the past; we insult it. The Victorians had not this sense of enlightenment, but they did enjoy a certain complacency in their escape from feudalistic government, religion, and social conditions. Carlyle tried to show, as did Ruskin later, that in some respects the past was superior to the present. An examination, he said, of certain aspects of twelfth-century life would prove this. With imagination as his guide, Carlyle tried to recreate the *fact* of the twelfth century as described in an old manuscript.

From this ideal the structure of *Past and Present* evolved naturally. The *Proem* sketches his purpose: to paint with all his skill a true picture of social conditions in England. The second book, *The An-*

cient Monk, is an etching, complete in itself, of a corner of twelfth-century England, with subtle emphasis upon its freedom from the social evils which beset modern England. The third book, *The Modern Worker,* depicts, in still clearer lines, nineteenth-century England, with many a bitter contrast to the earlier age. *Horoscope,* the fourth book, is concentrated Carlylean foreboding. Throughout *Past and Present* Carlyle points every moral for the present with an experience from the past—a method at variance somewhat with modern radicalism which is inclined to adorn its teachings by hypothetical lessons from an unknown future. In reversion to the past Carlyle outdoes the most conservative historians. "The Past," he says, "is a dim indubitable fact; the Future, too, is one, only dimmer."

The "dim, indubitable fact" in this case is for Carlyle a manuscript, written in monk-Latin of the twelfth century, *Chronica Jocelini de Brakelonda, de rebus gestis Samsonis Abbatis.* . . . Carlyle buried himself in this document, as he loved to do when writing history. Darwin's laugh at Carlyle's lack of scientific method took too little account, I sometimes think, of his patience in such researches. Portions of *The Ancient Monk* are excellent bits of scholarship. His picture of Bury St. Edmund is not romance, but reality fortified by authority. *The Ancient Monk* commands respect because it is truthful in both letter and spirit. A real danger in using the *Chronica* as the basis of a social pamphlet like *Past and Present* was pedantry. To brush the dust

from this document and let Jocelyn tell in translation
the story of the monastery would not be enough.
Carlyle was addressing not antiquarians but English
business men. He would hardly enhance the value
of his book by Latin syntax, however erudite. With
all its quaint literary flavour, a literal rendering of
the old story would appear heavy. But if pedantry
was the English reader's *bête noir*, it was also Carlyle's. It was a shoal, but Carlyle was never in great
danger of being wrecked upon it. He avoided any
imputation of pedantry by never ceasing to ridicule
the foibles of what he called bastard learning. Certainly no one was ever more scornful of the idiosyncrasies of scholarship. He is never tired of baiting
pedantry. Again and again, in speaking of the
Chronica, he jeers: "Giant Pedantry also will step
in with its huge *Dugdale* and other enormous *Mon-
asticons* under its arm." Or he indulges in a bur-
lesque pedantic note on *Beodric* and *weorth.* Or,
still more frequently, he lifts above such researches
the notice: "Dry Rubbish Shot Here."

If Carlyle's Scylla was pedantry, then his Charyb-
dis was dilettantism; and from this reef, too, he
resolutely steers his course. Englishmen were interested in the Middle Ages. Scott's novels were, perhaps, the most powerful influence. But much of this
interest was steeped in sentimentalism. Readers
looked back through a mist of romance. To many
it seemed as if the twelfth and thirteenth centuries
were one vast field of the cloth of gold on which
played at life crusaders, paladins, troubadours,

knights, and fair-haired maidens. "How glorious," thought the Victorian, and eagerly awaited the next Waverley novel. This same reader read later with something like a shock of disapproval more accurate tales of the early centuries: blood, hate, and suffering. Carlyle despised the sentimentalist as heartily as he did the pedant. This type of reader, he declared, believed gladly that the gold ring fished up from the river Trent belonged to the Countess of Leicester; and about the incident he spun a lovely romance. Why should it not have happened? Did not the Countess live in the age of chivalry?

Between the two attitudes towards the past Carlyle carves his own *via media;* he is never pedant, and never dilettante. For him the twelfth century is not dry rubbish, nor is it a glowing canvas of colour. He adheres, in the main, to fact, but into that fact he breathes imagination. The passage describing the election of Samson to the Abbotship is a beautiful illustration of Carlyle's method. In some respects this is but a translation, but imaginative touches here and there have somehow made, without sacrifice of truth, the long-forgotten event live again:

> "And now there remain," Carlyle's version goes, "on our List two only, Samson Subsacrista and the Prior. Which of these two? It were hard to say,—by Monks who may get themselves foot-gyved and thrown into limbo for speaking! We humbly request that the Bishop of Winchester and Geoffrey the Chance'lor may again enter, and help us to decide. 'Which do you want?'

asks the Bishop. Venerable Dennis made a speech, commending the persons of the Prior and Samson; but always in the corner of his discourse, *in angulo sui sermonis,* brought Samson in. . . . 'Either of them is good,' said venerable Dennis, almost trembling; 'but we would have the better, if it pleased God.' 'Which of the two *do* you want?' inquires the Bishop pointedly. 'Samson!' answered Dennis; 'Samson!' echoed all the rest that durst speak or echo anything."

Out of the remote past we feel again the emotion of that moment. Jocelyn had said: *"Et responsum est precise a pluribus et a majori parte, 'Volumus Samsonem,' nullo reclamante."* We are there, in Bury St. Edmund, with these earnest servants of Christ. Or with John Dice, one of the brethren, we look down secretly through the roof and see the Abbot bowed before the Sacred Body of St. Edmund himself; see him take the head between his hands: "He thus spake, groaning: 'Glorious Martyr, holy Edmund, blessed be the hour when thou wert born. Glorious Martyr. . . .'" The scene fades away and is buried in the centuries.

The total effect of many passages of this sort is a strong sense in the reader's mind of the reality of the life at Bury St. Edmund.

"Let us know always," Carlyle repeats, "that it *was* a world, and not a void infinite of gray haze with fantasms swimming in it."

And again he says: "That it is a *fact* and no dream, that we see it there, and gaze into the very eyes of it! Smoke rises daily from those culinary chimney-throats; there are living human beings there, who chant, loud-braying, their matins, nones, vespers."

Carlyle thus visualizes for his readers a society which, however circumscribed, may be compared, point for point, with that of the nineteenth century. Other social idealists have failed to create communities more real than this. The Utopias of Thomas More, of William Morris, or of Samuel Butler seem, by comparison, dreamy. These are projections of the imagination. But this portion of the twelfth century, even if limited and somewhat idealized, is real. It merited consideration in the 'forties; perhaps it does now. Throughout *The Ancient Monk* runs the implication that we should contrast the social organization of this monastic community with that of nineteenth-century England. "How silent," Carlyle says, "lie all Cotton trades and such like; not a steeple chimney yet got on end from sea to sea!" Landlord Edmund had few complaints from his tenants; or partridge seasons; or corn laws; or sliding scales.

Why should he have had? Society was still in its childhood. Landlord Edmund did not have to reckon with an Industrial Revolution, and for this reason, possibly, the contrast loses something of its force. But in the more abstract points of contrast Carlyle is stimulating. These are three familiar problems in Carlyle: government, religion, and leadership. As far as government is concerned, no one has ever accused Carlyle of definitely recommending a return to feudalism. On the other hand, it is clear that its principle of sovereignty was dearer to him than the ballot-box methods of the nineteenth

34

century. In Abbot Samson's microcosm there was what Carlyle regarded as genuine government. Bury St. Edmund is, in fact, a tiny corner of the ideal Carlylean government. Here was a segment at least of a working feudal aristocracy. This government took care of its people; the abomination of *laissez-faire* was still unborn. The business of a government, Carlyle used to shriek, is to govern. Under the feudal *régime* even a Gurth was entitled to his parings. Give the negro, Carlyle said, when questioned about the issues of the American Civil War, plenty of "sweet-pumpkin" and govern *him*. The theory of a government's responsibility to its people, yes, to each individual, was a truth that Carlyle kept on proclaiming. Certainly it may be found scores of times in *Past and Present*. Abbot Samson ruled and cared for those under him; among his people were no Chartisms or Manchester insurrections. Let the nineteenth century ponder on this sequence of cause and result: a government that governs and a contented people.

Yet still more remarkable at Bury St. Edmund was the religion; unquestionably it was a religion with faith. The religion of Carlyle's era has been wittily described as one which church members would be amazed to hear doubted or to see practised. Carlyle condemns the age's empty formulism in religion and also its abandonment of any faith whatsoever. The threnody by his disciple in *Modern Painters* on the substitution of despair for faith is a typical nineteenth-century lament. On all sides we encounter great thinkers doubtful or shaken in their ancient beliefs. "My brain was lightened," writes Clough, "when my tongue had said—'Christ is not risen.'" And Carlyle's own oft-repeated cry is: "We have forgotten God." But how different was religion at Bury St. Edmund. The faith of Abbot Samson was like that of the Apostles, silent, unquestioning. Moreover, under this rule eccentric religions did not appear. Carlyle notes that Samson did not have to deal with spectral Puseyisms or Methodisms. The religion of diseased introspection was unknown. There was then no "methodism with its eye forever turned on its own navel." Here were men who believed. Let the nineteenth century meditate also on this.

But, after all, the third point of contrast is most striking: the question of leadership. In that election of Abbot Samson everyone desired the right man—*nullo reclamante!* What Carlyle stresses is the attitude of the average man towards leadership. Carlyle did not expect either the British government or the British religion to change at once; he did not call out for institutional revolution. But he did believe that the type of leadership in the state could be altered, if light were vouchsafed Englishmen. Here Carlyle's appeal was again that of the moralist. Reform thyself. Make thyself a man better to be governed. What Carlyle did call out for was a spiritual revolution. Such a revolution would, he thought, bring England real leaders. Thus the great contrast between the twelfth and nineteenth centuries was not in institutions but in men. Carlyle evidently balances George III against Abbot Samson. The twelfth century worships a Samson or a St. Edmund; the nineteenth renders homage to a defender of the faith who is deaf, sightless, and insane; or a novelist; or a railroad engineer. In the earlier century the test of leadership is worth; in the later one it is royalty or the ballot-box.

For Carlyle is, of course, thinking of his old doctrine of "the hero." We must find "the hero," that wisest and best, that blend of vigour, silence, obedience, loyalty, with his surplusage of spiritual force, that—it must be confessed—somewhat elusive person. It sometimes seems as if "the hero" was concealed at the rainbow's end. But Carlyle persists in the search for him, and this romantic, political, economic tract called *Past and Present* is full of his presence. *The Ancient Monk* is another study in hero-worship. "The hero" is, after all, the chief touchstone used by Carlyle in testing the two contrasted centuries.

Carlyle never succeeded in convincing the nineteenth century of the practical value of this doctrine. And critics soon singled out the faults of the theory as set forth in *Past and Present,* as well as the other obvious defects of the book. It is not difficult to put one's finger on these. The practical application of *Past and Present* a child could impugn. One palpable error in analogy is that Samson's community is appreciably fewer in numbers than the twenty-seven millions of Englishmen for whom Carlyle wrote *Past and Present*. The laws of a monastery, cannot be transferred readily to a nation. Of course, Carlyle did not mean that the application should be made literally. He merely wished to suggest by example. But many thought that such was his purpose, and the influence of the idea was weakened by the misconception. Besides this, it was remarked that Carlyle had deliberately chosen a rather bright corner of the Middle Ages. There were other fractions of a feudal society coeval with Samson's community whose history would make different reading from that of Bury St. Edmund.

Moreover, in his arraignment of nineteenth-century religion Carlyle seemed to some to suggest the impossible: a return to a faith based on ignorance, to overlook the individualistic religious growth of seven centuries. Carlyle did not mean this either; but it was harmful to his purpose that people misunderstood him. Could the nineteenth century believe, as did the monks of St. Edmund, in a heaven like that of Thomas à Kempis? What Carlyle called diseased introspection was an inevitable by-product of the thought of Wycliffe, Luther, and Wesley, and of the scientific revelations of the new age. The perplexities were at least honest; not so much could be said for a reversion to blind mediæval faith. The nineteenth century ought, it is true, to have found better heroes. Democracy may not be the last stage of economic progress, and the ballot-box may be a hoax. Yet the eras of Peel and Disraeli could not select their leaders as the Bishop of Winchester did

38

Samson. Altogether there was hardly a detail in Samson's household management which could be adapted to modern England.

Such were typical criticisms of *Past and Present*. There is, of course, some truth in them. We may feel that Carlyle's constructive powers are under-estimated, but we must admit that he is more effective when he tells us what is the matter, than when he tells us what we shall do. But, in spite of such faults *Past and Present* has continued to exert an influence from 1843 to 1923. "There is nothing like it," said Arthur Hugh Clough. Its eloquence was partly responsible for Kingsley's novel, *Yeast*. It roused thousands of Englishmen from inertia to a fresh consideration of social conditions. The fierceness of the denunciation stung Philistine reformers out of their complacency. What if Carlyle did, as Henry James said, scold like an angry governess? He made men look about them more thoughtfully.

> "I hope," Carlyle wrote his mother, "it will be a rather useful kind of book. It goes rather in a fiery strain about the present condition of men in general, and the strange pass they are coming to; and I calculate it may awaken here and there a slumbering blockhead to rub his eyes and consider what he is about in God's creation."

This is the sum of the matter: a word from Carlyle was a call to action. He does battle against *laissez-faire*. "Ay," he said, "by God, Donald, we must help them to mend it!" He feels the joy of the conflict. Every sentence in *Past and Present* is a

39

plea against acquiescence. As Ruskin declares: "What can you say of Carlyle, but that he was born in the clouds and struck by the lightning?"

The interest that *Past and Present* has as a prophecy of social events which have now come to pass is evident if we examine *Horoscope.* Labour has always foretold its own future, sometimes reasonably, sometimes absurdly. The point of Carlyle's *Horoscope* lies in the definiteness of its predictions, and, in many cases, their accuracy. *Horoscope* is a protracted oracle. Carlyle prophesied especially the emancipation of the workman. The section is often nebulous, repetitive, and too rhapsodical in style, but, like most oracles, it has blest islets of the intelligible. We hear, for example, that "an actual . . . Industrial Aristocracy, real not imaginary Aristocracy, is indispensable and indubitable for us"; or that "we shall again have . . . instead of Mammon-Feudalism and unsold cotton shirts and preservation of the game, noble just Industrialism." These warnings are a little apocalyptic, but not so the following:

> "A question arises here: whether in some ulterior, perhaps some far distant stage of this 'Chivalry of Labour,' your Master-Worker may not find it possible and needful, to grant his workers permanent *interest* in his enterprise and theirs?"

This is a shrewd glimpse ahead. In fact, it is precisely because so many of Carlyle's hopes for labour are *faits accomplis,* that he seems in *Horoscope* to be in the position of one pleading for reforms already established. The conditions of labour

40

that are now matters of course Carlyle urged against opposition, and was regarded as visionary. Imagine a plea now for factory inspectors; for protection against typhus; or for some organization of labour. Of the labourers of England he asks despairingly: "Where are they to find a supportable existence?" Or, he cries as if hopeless: *"Cash-payment* is not the sole relation of human beings." Such amelioration as insurance for workingmen, model tenements for families, the possibility of arbitration of difficulties between workman and employer, occur to Carlyle, but doubtfully, as possible only in some millennium. But these are the commonplaces of today. They have come not by opportunist legislation—Carlyle's "Morrison's Pills"—but through thoughtful constructive government. Supervision of railroads, of factories, of living conditions has arrived in a measure exceeding Carlyle's hopes. But not in a manner exceeding his prophecies, for *Horoscope* predicts, "even at some far distant stage," these benefits.

Indeed, what the modern reader feels after reading this section with its forecasts of what "the Chivalry of Labour" must have is the tremendous strides made by labour since 1843 in securing its demands. It even seems as if a new *Past and Present* were needed, one which would assert somewhat the rights of the opponents of labour. No longer is it so necessary to denounce the gospels of mammonism, dilettantism, of oppression of workmen, of extortion by capital. The boot is on the other leg. Labour's emancipation is more complete than even Carlyle

41

would have guessed possible. Perhaps a book proclaiming the rights of the employer would be as pertinent today as was *Past and Present* in 1843. During the war there appeared in English newspapers, in adjacent columns, accounts of the imprisonment of petty offenders against the law, and of the release of notorious strike leaders. At this moment there is news of a strike which holds motionless almost every industrial activity in the British Isles. The union of labour parties of the world, without distinction of country, is partly achieved in the "Internationale." Carlyle's pious allusion to the land belonging to "the Almighty God, and to all His children of men that have ever worked well on it" is now an acknowledged principle among some millions of Communists, though indeed there is no certainty that God is included, or the test of working on the land required by this party. The wheel has come full circle. In three-quarters of a century men shrink less from the gospel of mammonism than from that of Bolshevism.

Carlyle was not, in any supernatural sense, a prophet. Yet apart from the mood of warning which is inseparable from him, he visualized with some clarity the future of labour. He thought constantly of the French Revolution, and honestly feared, unless labour were emancipated, that a similar fate might befall England. When he speaks of England "very ominously, shuddering, reeling, on the cliff's edge," he is more than rhetorical. He saw that things would change with "the millions who rejoiced in potatoes." Carlyle was responsible in no small measure for a strengthened belief in the worker's personal rights.

Kingsley's "Yeast"

Kingsley's "Yeast"

"THE . . . book," Carlyle wrote Kingsley of *Alton Locke,* "is definable as *crude;* to make the malt sweet, the fire should and must be slow; . . . the impression is of a fervid creation, still left half chaotic." Carlyle's criticism is truer of another novel of Kingsley's: *Yeast.* Someone has aptly characterized *Yeast* as "genius in a hurry." Nowhere else has Kingsley poured himself so recklessly over the printed page as in this novel written before his thirtieth birthday. *Yeast* lacks *genus:* it begins like a romance; proceeds as a political tract; and ends like a fairy-tale. But though nearly three-quarters of a century old, it still glows with Kingsley's ardour. The placid Victorian past becomes suddenly alive with fierce religious and social disputes. True, the turbulence of feeling in the book is somewhat disconcerting; and often its falsetto artistry provokes mirth; but its air of burning sincerity convinces. This strange novel is a strategic listening post for the conflicting movements of Victorian thought.

In action *Yeast* is a cross between a Platonic dialogue and a penny dreadful. The ribald little boy at the melodrama screaming for more murders would be content with Kingsley's extravagant and familiar devices. For it must be confessed that the Kingsley who declared himself nothing if not a priest loved a horrid tale. Lancelot's first meeting with Argemone recalls the story of the social nincompoop whose wont was to attract the attention of ladies by falling down stairs. Close by Argemone's high-church chapel Lancelot crashes from his horse, and suffers a timely concussion of the brain. In making Argemone nurse Lancelot back to life Kingsley observes almost the first of prehistoric literary traditions. The episode is his hearty version of the sprained-ankle motif.

This is melodrama, but it is Colonel Bracebridge, fox-hunter and courteous seducer, who really sets the lights low and the violins at *pizzicato*. He is guilty of no constructive piece of villainy, but his cleverness precludes his being virtuous. He is born out of his due time by at least a century, for in Fielding he would have been a hero. But in this Victorian company he is merely a soft-hearted radical who sins on claret. Kingsley's description of his death makes him a comic character. Certainly not all Victorians could have taken the following passage seriously. It is concerned with the letter which Bracebridge received immediately before he committed suicide, and which Lancelot read over the dead body of his friend:

> " 'How I loved you once! How I hate you now! But I have my revenge. *Your baby cried twice after it was born!*' Lancelot tore the letter into a hundred pieces and swallowed them."

The first love passage between Argemone and Lancelot is really a gentle religious controversy. In the first intimacy of love still unconfessed Lancelot ventures to assail those who were fighting for truth at Oxford:

46

" 'Oh, Mr. Smith,' she said, 'how can you dare to talk so of a liturgy compiled by the wisest and holiest of all countries and ages! . . . Oh,' she said hopefully, 'that you would but try the Church system! How you would find it harmonise and methodise every day, every hour for you! . . . Why not go to our vicar and open your doubts to him?' "

But brutal Lancelot would not try the vicar, for, as he states in a homily a page long, the vicar was inimical to Schiller, Böhme, and Carlyle! Yet he is not loth to talk with Argemone of love, and its denial of death. To Argemone's coy contention that the angelic life is single Lancelot demurs:

" 'How do we know that these angels, as they call them, if they be really persons, may not be united in pairs by some marriage bond, infinitely more perfect than any we can dream of on earth?' 'That is a very wild view, Mr. Smith, and not sanctioned by the Church,' said Argemone severely."

The lovers become more and more intellectual; in particular, the study of Homer binds them closely. The crescendo of sentiment reaches its height when Lancelot shows Argemone a drawing of his own, in Tennysonian tone, called the *Triumph of Woman*. Argemone drops a "single tear" over the figure of Woman, followed by a trusting gazelle and a wandering butterfly.

"And when she fancied that she traced in those bland aquiline lineaments, and in the crisp ringlets which floated like a cloud down to the knees of the figure,

47

some traces of her own likeness, a dream of a new
destiny floated before her,—she blushed to her very neck.
. . . 'You do not like it! I have been too bold,'—said
Lancelot, fearfully. 'Oh, no! no! It is so beautiful—
so full of deep wisdom! But—but—You may leave it.' "

Yeast is soaked in this kind of sentiment.

Argemone dies, and the result is a complete cessa-
tion of the action. The dialogues between the sym-
bolic characters become longer and more didactic.
The heroine and villain have vanished, and Kingsley
is at some pains to finish his tale. He is, indeed,
ridiculously like the author who got his hero at the
bottom of a well and lacked the proper literary hoist.
Like Sheridan's hero, it looks as if Lancelot would
have to crawl off the stage on his hands and knees.
What to do with Lancelot Smith? It is a problem,
but nobody would wish to have Kingsley leave *Yeast*
unended. A great unfinished novel may be left the
world by Dickens, but not by Kingsley. End it
Kingsley had to, and he did. He ended it by the
creation of a new character. by the unparalleled
Barnakill.

Barnakill is from Asia. His profession is unknown, and, even at his very first appearance, he is
occult enough to cause the reader considerable an-
noyance. As an avocation he affects banking, and
his outlook upon finance is, to say the least, cosmic.
He is, I think, literature's first transcendental business man. Barnakill has a knack of being found suddenly in odd places. He utters curious moral axioms;
he alludes cryptically to an unheard-of past and

future; and he is for ever displaying a weird omniscience concerning things both trivial and tremendous. Above all, Barnakill astounds and shames by his moral perfection. He bestows a sixpence upon Lancelot for lifting a trunk; thus Lancelot is taught the nobility of labour. Who is he? Not till the very end do we learn. Then Lancelot asks Barnakill about the underlying principle of their proposed ideal commonwealth. What is it to be? And Barnakill replies: " 'Jesus Christ—THE MAN.' "

> "He took Lancelot by the hand. A peaceful warmth diffused itself over his limbs; the droning of the organ sounded fainter and more faint; the marble monuments grew dim and distant; and, half unconsciously, he followed like a child through the cathedral door."

It is reasonably clear that Kingsley ended his novel with an incarnation of the Founder of Christianity.

The action of *Yeast* is certainly extraordinary, but to infer that Kingsley was less interested in action than character would be an error. His indifference to naturalness in his story was not due to greater concern over the thoughts and feelings of his characters. Most of these persons leave us cold except for interest in the beliefs to which they cling with such pious enthusiasm. Never depth of feeling in the face of the baffling facts of life, as in Thackeray; never the subtle growth of character, as in George Eliot. Each person is a doctrinaire, and Kingsley is interested in the doctrines. Every character is a mouthpiece for its creator, and it may be truly said

49

that from each comes, as has been remarked, "a roar worthy of that lion, Kingsley."

True, Argemone roars you as gently as the proverbial dove. She is as docile as the pet of Androcles. Yet she makes an excellent target for an enemy of Tractarianism. Argemone is important; it is difficult to see how without her Kingsley could have so harassed Puseyism. Like the writer of the doctoral thesis, Kingsley might almost dedicate his book to "the little woman who made this work possible." Argemone has been swept off her feet by the Oxford Movement. Her reading list is longer than Byron's and decidedly less heterodox. For Argemone is under the influence of *Credo in Newmannum:*

> "She was somewhat High Church in her notions, and used to go up every Wednesday and Friday to the chapel in the hills . . . for an hour's mystic devotion, set off by a little graceful asceticism."

A secret correspondence has prepared her for entrance into what Kingsley calls a quasi-Protestant nunnery. At the last instant Argemone recedes from her decision, for she realizes her love for Lancelot. Kingsley exults in the thought that covert Romanism cannot triumph over a real love of body and spirit. With delight he dwells on the defeat of the rickety windmill of sham-popery. Through Argemone Kingsley tries to show the sin and futility of ultra-Romanism in the Anglican Church.

Equally definite is a phase of thought elucidated

through Argemone's lover, Lancelot Smith. This
hero is an amazing blend of muscle and metaphysics,
and his mind is a storm-center for the religious doubt
of the day. The conventional beacons of faith
Lancelot hardly sees. He has, if such a conquest is
possible, mastered German philosophy; and Carlyle
is a passion. The orthodox churches he will not
tolerate, because of their casuistry and their impatience of the physical needs of men. Lancelot
professes to be a splendid and unregenerate animal.
He stamps upon the earth and delights to run his
race. All the healthy Kingsleyan virtues are his;
and he is easily recognizable as a brother to Amyas
Leigh, and other characters in less ecclesiastical
novels of Kingsley's.

Especially does Lancelot love the dust of combat
with what he considers the unmanly aspects of
religion. Theology has made the Church a cold ab-
straction. He writes dreary letters to Luke, the
Tractarian curate, denouncing effeminacy in the Anglican and Catholic Churches. The pale, peaked
faces of holy men stir in him depths of fury, and
he ascribes the easy conquest of the animal nature
to its fundamental absence. At the nadir of Lancelot's unrest Tregarva, the Methodist gamekeeper,
shows him the misery of the English agricultural
poor. Lancelot's disgust for altars, on which you
could not see the Christ for saints, deepens. The
true religion, he concludes, must involve increasing
care for social betterment. Here, at least, is a man's
work; to it Lancelot consecrates his life. The char-

acter is obviously a symbol of the spiritual dissatisfaction of England's young men—and of the ideal remedy! Lancelot is, I believe, the best sketch in literature of Kingsley's "muscular Christian," or of the "Christian Socialist." Note the name of Lancelot Smith, a delightful sample of Kingsley's naïveté in novel construction. Lancelot is a nineteenth-century knight-errant, but he is also *Smith,* of the Smiths; of the stock and stem of everyday Englishmen. He is a champion for and of the common people.

We of the next century, the incredible twentieth, think our age the crepuscular time before the birth of a new order. But Kingsley thought this of the nineteenth century. In the preface to the First Edition of *Yeast* he declares that he has tried to express truly popular notions of the social and religious order. Aptly enough the caption of one of Kingsley's poems might be made the title of *Yeast,—The Dead Church.* This is a basic idea in the book, whether one thinks of Argemone's pathetic neo-Catholicism or Lancelot's bitter echo from Carlyle: "We have forgotten God."

Always this despair is closely linked with antagonism towards the Catholic Church. Kingsley's is the eternal opposition of the Protestant to the Catholic theory of authority. The security and happiness of Luke, after going to Rome, he cannot endure. Kingsley's whole life, I occasionally think, was a rough and ready struggle against doubt; therefore, what he cannot endure in Catholics is their certainty. The

letters to Luke, denouncing Catholicism, have their
prototypes in actual letters of Charles Kingsley.
Sometimes it seems as if this resentment has its origin
in yearning after the faith for which he was tem-
peramentally unfitted. "I have been through it," he
says. "I have longed for Rome, and boldly faced
the consequences of joining Rome."

Naturally, Kingsley is hardly less hostile towards
the party seeking to deprotestantize the Anglican
Church. Weak men such as Luke were likely to
find it a half-step to Rome. Thus the vicar who
lays siege to Argemone is an unwitting sophist, and
is represented as having marked leanings towards the
ancient church. But Kingsley's real accusation against
the Oxford Movement was that it created new
wounds in the Church, when all her might was needed
to fight real and sinister enemies within the fold.
Lancelot is estopped from embracing Christian
Socialism earlier because his brain has been confused
by the unintelligible heresies and hair-splitting con-
troversies of the ecclesiastics. Similarly, Argemone's
vapid devotions in the woodland chapel disappear
in the face of the real issue of helping the wretches
in England's countryside. That Kingsley was blunder-
ingly right in believing that chicanery existed between
the neo-Catholics and Rome may not be a defensible
position. Certainly Newman saw to it that this attitude ended disastrously for Kingsley. But that the
discussion of æsthetic practices, or even of dogma,
was trivial compared with the immediate relief of
the misery of the poor—this is tenable ground, and

constituted in *Yeast*, as elsewhere, Kingsley's strongest contention against the Oxford Movement.

The central current of thought in *Yeast* is concerned with Christian Socialism. Tregarva interprets the misery of the country as in *Alton Locke* Sandy Mackaye depicts the anguish of the city. In these episodes Lancelot is merely a Socratic questioner, and Tregarva's long responses are like a Kingsleyan social pamphlet. The kinds of oppression are not wholly familiar, but Kingsley convinces by sheer vehemence and passion; and the twentieth-century reader finds himself connecting by secret conduits the suffering of 1850 and the unrest of 1923. Is the picture too sordid to be truthful? Let there make answer the *Corn Law Rhymes* of Ebenezer Elliott, the lyrics of Hood, or the *Autobiography of a Chartist,* by Thomas Cooper. Although it is easy to smile at England's Jeremiahs, the truth remains that she has been often on the brink of social revolution. And one of these times was the day of the Chartist. *Yeast* is a practical advertisement of the cause of Christan Socialism. Against the troubles described in *Yeast* Frederick Denison Maurice and Charles Kingsley had united as the first Christian Socialists. The mode of battle was the old one of the Puseyites, the tract. The new *Tracts for the Times* were for the workingmen of England, and were called *Politics for the People.* The organization of the Christian Socialists was complex, but their platform was simple: the application of "the practical principles of Christianity to the purposes of trade and industry."

Rossetti, once passing an election meeting, is said to have remarked idly: "Well, I suppose someone will get in." The artist-poet turned to what he considered the more enduring interests of art and literature. And I see no reason why a student of the Victorians should examine *Yeast* so precisely, if it were filled merely with religious or political transiencies. But it mirrors, too, the literary tendencies of its time. The stamp of the exemplars of the literature of 1850 is upon the book. Such influences and literary inter-relations have a certain interest even today, not only for the red-blooded hunter who spends the summer in the library gunning for sources, but also for the critic of significant nineteenth-century prose and poetry. Kingsley was an imitative writer. His great model in poetry was Tennyson; in prose Carlyle. Everywhere in *Yeast* is apparent Kingsley's enormous debt to Carlyle. References to him are frequent, and the very spirit of the book is Carlyle's. If *Alton Locke* was inspired by the *French Revolution*, certainly *Yeast* was directly affected by *Past and Present*. In its abruptness, its eloquence, and its sincerity it is Carlylean.

Yeast's failure to hold its own among literary productions of the 'fifties is due chiefly to the fact that many of its problems were accidental and ephemeral. Though the fundamental political and religious questions still torment us, the particular issue of Poor Law Relief is no longer vital. Kingsley, foolishly enough, stressed not the deeper issue, but the topic of the day. Art always avenges itself

55

upon the artist who uses his gift for a temporary end, and Kingsley's *Yeast* pays this penalty. Witch-burning is not now a menace, but men will continue to read *The Scarlet Letter* because it considers the unsolved problems of the human soul, and thus has eternal interest. *Yeast* was always, in the literary sense, justly perishable.

But students of Victorian literature will still read this potpourri. They will be sensible of its anomalies, its fallacies, its roughness, and its forgotten prejudices. They will be amused at this singular combination of Platonic dialogue, tract, sermon, diatribe, and ballad, but they will understand the Victorians better, and so think their reading worth while.

"In homely English," Kingsley concludes in his Epilogue, "I have given my readers *Yeast;* if they be what I take them for, they will be able to bake with it themselves."

Two Victorian Boyhoods

Two Victorian Boyhoods

THE boy is sometimes father of the man, but more often he is the son of his own generation. His ideals may mould the future, but they are born of the past. To care greatly to become a statesman, a poet, or a man, is to care for those things of the past which belong to leadership, poetry, or manhood. All thoughts, all passions, all delights that stir the frame of boyhood are criticisms upon the past. Ruskin's *Two Boyhoods* is apposite. Giorgione in brilliant Venice and Turner in dim Covent Garden gather up the traditions of their peoples.

So do Victorian boyhoods. Catholicism, Evangelicalism, Socialism, Rationalism, a very riot of "isms" —"infinite jumble and mess and dislocation," groans Carlyle!—were all whirled in a crucible and poured into the minds of wretched little Victorians. How the juvenilia of the nineteenth century add their treble to the philosophical burden! Diaries of the callow period are tiny pools churned and darkened by the main currents of thought. Dear little Tory, Ruskin's chief hope in life is "to see Kings." Kingsley (*ætat.* four) composes a nursery sermon with the final assurance: "Yea, ye generation of vipers!" In his teens Tom Huxley speculates on the origin of colors at sunset; at about the same age Walter Besant wriggles in the family pew, while from the pulpit is droned, hours long, the rose-tinted message of John Calvin.

Of all Victorian autobiographies, two are at once

most like and most unlike, most characteristic and most extraordinary. These two books are the *Autobiography of John Stuart Mill,* and *Father and Son,* now known to have been written by Edmund Gosse. To allude to these books as *Two Victorian Boyhoods* is whimsical: Mill's boyhood was Georgian, and his book is of manhood; Gosse's book is of boyhood, and his manhood is modern. Yet the boyhoods of both men were profoundly Victorian. One should not think of Victorianism as a list of dates, but rather as various and complex states of mind. Though Mill was thirty-one years old at the accession of the Queen, he was victimized by a particular trend of Victorian thought; and though Mr. Gosse is now alive and has recently given us his humane *Life of Swinburne,* he was for many years enslaved by yet another system. The imprisoner of Mill's youthful mind was fanatical rationalism; of Gosse's, fanatical religion. These two powerful modes of thought, like Balin and Balan, fought not only all enemies, but each other. Chesterton's name for the grapple of the two forces is the Victorian Compromise. Understand them, and you may apprehend some of the intellectual secrets of the age.

It is more than a paradox to say that the two different boyhoods were similar. Both boys were the sons of distinguished fathers. The historian of India needs no appraisal; and but for *Omphalos,* which strove to reconcile the last chapter of geology with the first chapter of Genesis, the elder Gosse would have retained the respect of Darwin and Hux-

ley. Both fathers were supremely proprietary: Mill
and Gosse felt not the stimulus but the imposition
of an education. Their boyish minds were *forced*
into the paternal thought-grooves. Each education
was severe, and, though not equally so, each was
narrow. At the age of three, Mill was coolly learning Greek vocables; at about the age of four,
Gosse was tearfully memorizing interminable hymns,
psalms, and chapters of scripture. Here, in lowest
terms, were Hellenism and Hebraism. Mill was
forbidden to read the Bible; Gosse was denied all
else. Neither curriculum suggests a liberal education.
Of the enriching experience of being merely a boy,
neither Mill nor Gosse had an intimation. James
Mill considered the society of healthy, apple-eating
boys a species of decadence. And Gosse draws a
black vignette of himself with "Benny," a "play-
mate": the two children wandered up and down the
garden wondering how to play! Years later Mill
remarked to Caroline Fox that he had no notion of
a normal boyhood; and no such confession is required
from the author of *Father and Son*. Another
similarity, of importance to the world: they both
achieved intellectual independence; and, in the case
of Gosse, this was nothing less than the end of
spiritual bondage.

Victorian propriety is a byword that misleads; it
connotes restraint. But no age was more aggres-
sively dogmatic than the Victorian. In politics there
was war without quarter.

Studies in Victorian Literature

> "I have no hesitation in saying," Mr. Gladstone told Mr. G. W. E. Russell, "that if the repeal of the Corn Laws had been defeated, or even retarded, we should have had a revolution."

Charles Kingsley feared ("hoped" would be hyperbole) a revolution in 1848. Science, too, was an incredible irritant:

> "O ye men of science, ye men of science," sighed a clergyman, "leave us our ancestors in paradise, and you may have yours in Zoölogical gardens!"

If Newman's *Loss and Gain* is realism, then Charles Reading's anguished farewell to his mother, when he turns Catholic, was a typical *mise en scène*. Yet Newman, if one trusts Carlyle, had only the brain of a full-grown rabbit. Pusey said man was a spiritual humpback, deformed by sin, but others thought him a likable person without any religion at all. When Lord Melbourne was compelled to listen to a sermon on sin, he declared indignantly: "Things have come to a pretty pass when religion is allowed to invade the sphere of private life!" There were fewer stake-burnings than in preceding centuries, but more heart-burnings, and just as much bitterness. People did not disagree with their friends; they converted them; and the damning of enemies to uncomfortable eternities was a postulate in every charitable creed. The households, both of Mill and Gosse, shared this sweet intolerance; the vivid difference lay merely in the objects at which it was aimed.

Mill's father was a spiritual descendant of the eighteenth-century rationalists. His mentor and complete friend was Jeremy Bentham. Surely young Mill's prattle was of syllogisms. I fancy him, like Hercules, in the cradle strangling with logical baby fingers serpentine irrationalisms. But motivating every thought of the elder Gosse was John Calvin. Long before Edmund Gosse's birth he was "dedicated to the Lord." Mill, the eldest son of the political economist, was as truly dedicated to Reason. Robespierre's consecration to the goddess at the Feast of the *Être Supreme* was more scenic but less sincere than John Stuart Mill's. Thus the guardian angels of Reason and Religion were appointed for two Victorian boys.

"I was brought up," says Mill, "from the first without any religious belief, in the ordinary acceptation of the term."

"I read," says Gosse, as if antiphonally, "the Bible every day, and at much length; also . . . a book of incommunicable dreariness, called Newton's *Thoughts on the Apocalypse*. . . . I made a sort of playful compact with my Mother that if I read aloud a certain number of pages out of *Thoughts on the Apocalypse,* as a reward I should be allowed to recite 'my own favorite hymns.' "

Imagine James Mill's opinion of such a compact!

For, says his son, "he impressed upon me from the first, that the manner in which the world came into existence was a subject on which nothing was known: that the question, 'Who made me?' cannot be answered, because we have no experience or authentic information from which to answer it; and that any answer only throws the difficulty a step further back, since the question immediately presents itself, 'Who made God?'"

This blasphemous question was never raised by the Gosse family. Who would debate an axiom?

"My parents," Gosse says, "founded every action, every attitude, upon their interpretation of the Scriptures, and upon the guidance of the Divine Will, as revealed to them by direct answer to prayer."

The child soon thought of Him as a persistent Guest, and one rather difficult to entertain. He was a literal Fourth never absent from the family group. At prayers, of course, but also at the breakfast table, in the walks about London, there *"He"* was. Not cheerful company, either:

"When my mother had tucked me up in bed, and had heard me say my prayer, and had prayed aloud on her knees at my side, and had stolen downstairs, noises immediately began in the room. There was a rustling of clothes, and a slapping of hands, and a gurgling, and a sniffing, and a trotting. These horrible muffled sounds would go on, and die away, and be resumed; I would pray God to save me from my enemies."

O *dies iræ!* Painted hell! What relish to burn all mankind save the "Plymouth Brethren"! Or, if an Anabaptist, what joy to burn all mankind, especially the "Plymouth Brethren." Here, at last, is the true

Setebos.   Here is a God who wearies not in torturing
little children:

> "If anyone was ill, it showed that 'the Lord's hand
> was extended in chastisement,' and much prayer was
> poured forth in order that it might be explained to the
> sufferer, or to his relations, in what he or they had
> sinned.   People would, for instance, go on living over
> a cesspool, working themselves into an agony to discover
> how they had incurred the displeasure of the Lord."

But among the Mills, there was no chimera of a
flaming pit.

> "Think," James Mill was wont to say, ". . . of a
> being who would make a Hell—who would create the
> human race with the infallible foreknowledge, and there-
> fore with the intention, that the great majority of them
> were to be consigned to horrible and everlasting tor-
> ment."

Spectral religion made Gosse's boyhood a night-
mare.   It is difficult for the modern reader of *Father
and Son* to see how he preserved his mind.   In the
zoölogical age of H. G. Wells you qualify your
church membership, if cornered on that point, by
the adjective "nominal."   "I am not much interested
in religion," says a "nominal" friend of mine, and
his mild satire is echoed in earnest from innumerable
American country-clubs.   Family prayers are as
fashionable as the hoopskirt or the one-horse shay,
and grace before meat is the unspoken: "There being
no minister present, let's thank God and sit down."

Accordingly, we doubt first the sincerity and then the sanity of the Gosses.

Every dedication of a child to the Lord in the 'fifties must have won another grin from Moloch. With the child's first breath the father began to prepare him for communion with "the saints," that is, the "Plymouth Brethren." Gosse's father insisted upon instant spiritual efflorescence. He tilled the new soul intensively, passionately. "Sacrificial" whippings, hymns of humiliation, the "jealous God," a "personal Devil," and the "blood of Jesus,"—all accelerated the state of grace.

Indeed, this apprenticeship nearly brought the final beatitude promised to the elect. This period of Gosse's life is a study in nerves. A bit of plum-pudding, furtively eaten on a dismal Christmas day, nearly solved the problem of Eternity:

> "Shortly I began to feel that pain inside which in my frail state was inevitable, and my conscience smote me violently. At length I could bear my spiritual anguish no longer, and bursting into the study I called out: 'Oh! Papa, Papa, I have eaten of flesh, offered to idols!'"

On another occasion young Gosse overheard a discussion concerning his future:

> "I shut my eyes, and lay quite still, in order to escape conversing with them, and they spoke to one another. 'Ah, poor lamb,' Kate said trivially, *'he's* not long for this world; going home to Jesus, he is,—in a jiffy, I should say by the look of 'un.' But Susan answered: 'Not so. I dreamed about 'un, and I know for sure that

66

he is to be spared for missionary service. . . .' 'Yes,' Susan went on, with solemn emphasis, 'he'll bleed for his Lord in heathen parts, that's what the future have in store for *'im.'* "

Gosse was spared. When ten years old, after an ecstatic public baptism, he was admitted "as an adult" to the saints. His was now a special ministry: it was his duty to speak unceasingly "in season and out of season of the blood of Jesus." This fanatical religious life continued throughout Gosse's early manhood.

Meanwhile (at a corresponding age) Mill was plundering Greek and Latin literature. His province included all history and philosophy. In his eighth year he had begun Latin, and before he was twelve he had made Aristotle's *Rhetoric* into synoptic tables. Simultaneously, he *wrote* histories and verse. Henry Gosse developed, he thought, his son's soul; James Mill gave part of his life to his son's intellect. As a result, he was able to make the astounding and, perhaps, truthful statement that John Stuart Mill surpassed his contemporaries intellectually by a quarter of a century. How ironic that each father scorned the concern dearest to the other! Of his religious training, Mill says: "I am thus one of the very few examples, in this country, of one who has, not thrown off religious belief but never had it." While Gosse, save for a little science and other casual details, was taught nothing except Christ crucified. He was nearly in his teens when James Sheridan Knowles explained to him the meaning of the word

67

"stage," and mentioned—for the first time in his hearing—the name of Shakespeare. Of the logic, psychology, and philosophy on which Mill was nurtured, he had not heard. Each father indulged his prejudices, and in both sons the minds were bent.

But it is not proposed to compare the knowledge or the quality of mind of these two different and, strictly speaking, not contemporary men, but rather the ψυχή behind each boyhood. Reiteration is pardonable: as the *motif* of Gosse's youth was religion, that of Mill's was reason. It was not that Mill was made to read thoroughly; the point is that he was made to think. He once used the word "idea." "What is an *idea?*" demanded James Mill, turning upon him sharply. The staccato question was a symbol. Then and always Mill had to find out what things were.

The religion of the Gosses inspired a deep emotional life. Gosse's boyhood was hallowed by a real tenderness. The certitude of God sometimes brings peace without stint. Gosse's picture of his mother is lovely:

> "My Father and Mother," he says, "lived so completely in the atmosphere of faith, and were so utterly convinced of their intercourse with God, that, so long as that intercourse was not clouded by sin, to which they were delicately sensitive, they could afford to take the passing hour very lightly. . . . My Mother was sometimes extremely gay, laughing with a soft, merry sound. What I have since been told of the guileless mirth of nuns in a convent has reminded me of the gaiety of my parents during my early childhood."

Their table-talk was a naïve mélange of science and holy writ:

> "We were sitting at family prayers, on a summer morning, I think in 1855, when through the open window a brown moth came sailing. My Mother immediately interrupted the reading of the Bible by saying to my Father, 'O! Henry, do you think that can be *boletobia?*' My Father rose up from the sacred Book, examined the insect, which had now perched, and replied: 'No! it is only the common Vapourer, *orgygia antiqua,*' resuming his seat, and the exposition of the Word, without any apology or embarrassment."

But James Mill's rationalization of life included his wife and children. He owned to destructive theories concerning the family unit. Objects of respect he aimed to make his children; objects of affection they were not. Mill does not shrink from an indictment. In the chapter on his father he says: "The element which was chiefly deficient in his moral relation to his children was that of tenderness."

In these boyhoods are exhibited two Victorian tendencies: extreme Rationalism and extreme Religion. Each was a false ideal. It was a peculiarity of the Victorians to mistake a coign of vantage for the summit of the mountain. They created cults and called them perfection. The two boyhoods attest this. For nearly thirty years Matthew Arnold pleaded with his countrymen not to emphasize the means of attaining perfection, whether reason, religion, or railroads, but Perfection itself. Not by the syllogism nor by the blood of Jesus in season and out of season shall we overtake Truth. When the pursuers become frantic, the mysterious goddess veils her face and flees. Perhaps she laughs. Certainly she smiles at devotees who immolate in her name boys like John Stuart Mill and Edmund Gosse.

The Poetical Reputation of Matthew
Arnold

The Poetical Reputation of Matthew Arnold

In December, 1922, occurred the one-hundredth anniversary of the birth of Matthew Arnold. Since his death more than a third of a century has passed, and it is nearly three-quarters of a century since the publication of his first poems—*Poems by A.*, that first slender sheaf was named, when it appeared in 1849. It was later known that "A." was "Mat" Arnold, "the leader of the younger English poets." It gives one a start now to realize that Arnold, whom I recently heard an American novelist call "a Victorian fossil," was once regarded as a person quite new, a modern, in fact! But time has done its work, and has changed the leader of the younger English poets into an ancient Victorian. *Quantum mutatus.*

It must be admitted that even in his own day Arnold's poetry was imperfectly appreciated. Much more difficult is it to estimate its influence today. Most of us could sketch, if put to it, the poetical fortunes of Wordsworth or Byron or Shelley. To trace Arnold's is not so easy. In the early 'sixties, if we trust Edward Cook's *Literary Recreations,* a printer remarked petulantly: "Who is this Matthew Arnold, and how many more columns of him is the editor going to shovel up?" And now, in the early 'twenties, one may hear an ironical echo from students: "Who is Matthew Arnold? Why read *him?*" Yet we do turn to him, more faithfully than is supposed. And it was not wholly obituary en-

73

thusiasm which inspired the *Nation* to say in 1888: "There was probably no name in current English literature better known to the present generation than his." What does Matthew Arnold's poetry mean to us after three-quarters of a century?

The fact that Arnold has been partly forgotten is not merely another illustration for Solomon's text —another *sic transit gloria*. Arnold has been superseded, of course, by other "younger poets." He wrote less, and, on the whole, not so well as Tennyson and Browning, and so was more perishable. But I take it that our indifference to such poetry as Arnold's is especially characteristic of the twentieth century's attitude towards the literary past. No century, I believe, has ever had less reverence for the past than ours. Gray, like Arnold, came down to a succeeding age with a very thin volume of verse, but the nineteenth century did not ask who Gray was. It knew, although it may not have read his poetry. But what is more fashionable in the twentieth century than a sneer at a Victorian poet? Even Browning societies are somewhat spent. There now exists a group of poets who are frankly scornful of Shelley and Keats. To many, Victorian poetry, like Victorian furniture, or Victorian morals, is a target for pleasantry.

Nevertheless, the secret laws of the enduring in poetry are not stayed. We believe that. Jests concerning the proper Tennyson or the academic Arnold give no clue to the place of their poetry in the minds of even the scoffers. Thoughtful men and women still read Victorian poetry. How much is the question; I should say, in thinking of my own friends, a great deal. But, more definitely, now that almost seventy-five years have elapsed since the *Poems by A.* was reviewed by the London *Times,* what answer can be given to these annoyed queries of the printer and student, "Who is Matthew Arnold?" Who reads now the poetry which is, supposedly, "a criticism of life"? Who is by this poetry, like Mycerinus, "calm'd, ennobled, comforted, sustain'd"? What have been the varying fortunes of Matthew Arnold's poetry from 1849 to 1923?

Arnold himself was interested in the question. Although a poet only by avocation, he took thought for the morrow. It is interesting to know that he was confident that his poetry would endure. In fact he prophesies, and the truth of his prophecy is now examinable:

> "My poems represent," he wrote his mother in 1869, "on the whole, the main movement of mind of the last quarter of a century, and thus they will probably have their day as people become conscious to themselves of what that movement of mind is, and interested in the literary productions that reflect it. It might be fairly urged that I have less poetical sentiment than Tennyson, and less intellectual vigour and abundance than Browning; yet, because I have perhaps more of a fusion of the two than either of them, and have more regularly applied that fusion to the main line of modern development, I am likely enough to have my turn, as they have had theirs."

If Arnold meant that he would ever enjoy such

75

popularity as that of Tennyson or Browning, he was, of course, mistaken. In this sense he never had his "turn." No one ever declared of Arnold what Walter Besant said, while he was at Cambridge, of the poems of Tennyson, or Kingsley: that they "were in everybody's hands." Nor would Besant have remarked of Arnold what he said and what many felt concerning Tennyson: "Of all the men of our century I would rather have been Tennyson than any other man whatever." Swinburne, as noted later, commented on the familiarity of Eton boys with Arnold's poetry, but it cannot really be said of him, as Arnold himself declared concerning Swinburne in 1870, that he was "the favourite poet of the young men at Oxford." But the first sentence of Arnold's prophecy is suggestive. He was aware that his poetry epitomized a "main movement of mind." No one can deny this. Studies of Victorian thought cannot neglect Matthew Arnold. And more and more his poetry seems to express, not a special phase of thought, but a blending of many phases. In Tennyson's poetry we find an orthodox idealism which, after all, was not abreast of the most progressive Victorian thought. The blameless King Arthur and the one increasing purpose represent only one aspect of Victorian conviction. And Victorian thought was, at best, a maze of doubt and conflicting beliefs. The reflections in Arnold's poetry of what men were thinking are less piously hopeful than those in Tennyson's, but they are truer. Mirrored, directly or indirectly, in the poetry of Arnold are the grapple of science and the church; the social friction; the fierce industrialism; the desperate appeals for leadership (to Goethe, to Wordsworth, to Byron, to anyone!); in sum, the spiritual confusion which left so deep a mark upon Arnold himself. As Mr. Henry Nevinson said recently, Arnold

"represents exactly the mood of the serious and religiously minded men whose faith in dogmatic Christianity was shaken by the natural science and biblical criticism of seventy years ago."

To record this main movement of mind honestly was the achievement of Matthew Arnold's poetry.

The realization that Arnold's poetry reproduces the consciousness of the age has, of course, come very gradually. We can trace the growth of the conviction that it does this in the reviews, in the opinions of contemporaries, and in the history of the editions of the poetry. Most of Arnold's poetry was written between 1849 and 1870; during these years appeared *The Strayed Reveller, and Other Poems; Empedocles on Etna;* the *Poems* of 1853 and 1855; and the *New Poems* of 1867. Not once was there a popular recognition of this poetry, either in England or America. Arnold's poetical popularity, to adapt his own description of miracles, simply did not occur. Not a meteor, like Byron, he was rather a distant planet, destined to remain long unregarded, but perhaps more steadfast—who knows?—than brighter stars. Certainly the new planet was not considered important by the reviewers of the 'fifties. *Poems by A.* was not widely reviewed. The general impression was that this new poetry had excellence of finish, but was weak in morals, and in interest. The critic for *Fraser's Magazine* declares that "there is no place in literature for the *New Sirens,* or for sleepy melancholy meditations . . . on a 'Gipsy Child.'"

> "What," so runs the malediction, "in the name of all grim earnest do we want with 'Resignation, to Fausta,' a yawn thirteen pages long, with which the volume finally falls fast asleep, and vanishes in a snore? Resignation! To what?"

The critic then preaches at "A," as well as at all other poetic upstarts. "A." is warned that

> "he will not escape unscorched, . . . if he chooses to trifle with the public by verifying dreamy, transcendental excuses for laziness, for want of an earnest purpose and a fixed creed."

This does not sound like having one's turn. It is possibly the same critic who, five years later, denounces the ending of *Sohrab and Rustum.* "Who cares," he asks, "whither the Oxus goes, or what becomes of it?" When *Empedocles on Etna* appeared in 1852, the *Times* was the aggressor. This critic cannot endure Arnold. He is "disgusted with the world; a state of mind with which we have no sympathy whatever." Similarly, the *North British Review* points out that Arnold is guilty of "an indolent selfish quietism."

The Poetical Reputation

So much for awaking to find oneself famous. This was not to be Arnold's experience. But even in this mid-century obscurity some critics felt Arnold's power. One even remarked that *"Mycerinus* was a fragment worthy of Tennyson"—although this may have been dubious praise to a somewhat envious Arnold. And the London *Times,* in recommending Arnold's poetry, complains that "to the generality of readers he remains unknown, while the world is full of the praises of far inferior writers." These reluctant amenities, however, are less significant than the interest of certain contemporaries. In 1856 Coventry Patmore writes William Allingham, not thinking that his arrangement of poets is climactic: "The future belongs to you and me and Matthew Arnold." It is clear that there began at once an infiltration of Arnold's poetry into the imperishable part of English literature. This process has, moreover, persisted, in the face of antagonism and indifference until today the person who prefers Arnold's poetry to Tennyson's is no longer regarded as whimsical.

Arnold was destined, however, to be widely known first of all for his prose. Except for the year 1867 his poetry ceased. No chance now for the reviewers to decry the skimble-skamble stuff of the son of Doctor Arnold. Instead, Mr. Frank Newman, he, according to Carlyle, of "the mildest pious enthusiasm," found himself the object of a sad and pitying smile; and he became keenly conscious that his fame as a translator of Homer was unsafe.

79

Arnold's essay, *On Translating Homer,* appeared in
1861—a first thrust at British complacency. *Culture
and Anarchy* followed eight years later. Then came
the nettles of *Friendship's Garland,* an irritant that
inspired the Philistine with amused chagrin. In
America the swallow torments the crow. On pine
tree or in flight he deftly pecks at the waistcoat of
the black plutocrat. Ruffled, the sleek Philistine of
birds utters loud British caws. Through Arnold
the English business-man acquired a similar enemy.
Carlyle had attacked him in "Bobus Higgins," the
sausage-maker certain that England's greatness depended upon her industries, but Arnold was far more
dexterous, more incisive. Besides, the Philistine
found reply futile. Useless to call him "a priest of
the kid-glove persuasion"; useless to vilify him; useless to answer, like Mr. Frederic Harrison, with
adroit banter. The satirist read all the replies; his
aplomb was perfect. And at Mr. Harrison's *Culture: A Dialogue* he laughed till he cried. "Damn
this fop," groaned a Philistine, "can nobody annoy
him?"

In writing prose Arnold had declared war on the
Philistine. This was his definite purpose. But apart
from this, it is not surprising that he continued to
turn out volume after volume of prose. It made him
known everywhere. His poetry was greeted with
silence; his prose was received, like the death of
Balder, with shrieks from every living thing. Arnold
knew that he had hit the mark; he followed public
opinion closely. If we look into his letters we find

him smiling and delighted at his notoriety. He writes Lady de Rothschild about the favourable notice of his essays in the *Westminster Review,* but humorously deprecates "the hideous title of 'Professor.'" Two years later he is charmed by a eulogy in the *North American Review,* and in 1867 he gossips with his mother about the familiarity of his name in the newspapers:

> "The *Saturday,*" he says, "had a reference to me which I liked better than that in the *Spectator.* Lord Lytton's mention of me was, as you may suppose, a pleasant surprise."

Meanwhile, as he is having dinner at Goschen's, he hears the word "Philistine" used at least a hundred times. Disraeli, too, goes out of his way to promise him a brilliant future,* and at Darmstadt the Princess Alice is fascinated by *Culture and Anarchy.*

Thus Arnold was inclined to encourage the assertion that he would be known to posterity primarily as a writer of prose. He assumed quite naturally the rôle of the critic of society. Simultaneously with the interest he inspired, Arnold annoyed his readers

---

* Arnold describes the incident in a letter to his mother, written on January 28, 1864. Disraeli said "he thought he had seen me somewhere, and I said Lord Houghton had introduced me to him eight or nine years ago at a literary dinner among a crowd of other people. 'Oh yes, I remember,' he said, and then he went on: 'at that time I had a great respect for the name you bore, but you yourself were little known. Now you are well known. You have made a reputation, but you will go further yet. You have a great future before you, and you deserve it.'" Reference is made to this incident and to Disraeli's admiration for Arnold in the biographies of Disraeli.

by his urbane assurance of manner—his "I—I—I—
Das grosse Ich," as the *Saturday Review* described
it; but apart from this "moral smelling bottle,"—
another newspaper phrase—the important journals
regarded him as early as 1865 as "a critic with a
very high idea of the function of criticism." "He
is," says the *Westminster Review,* "in spite of some
faults, the very best critic we possess." It is interesting to observe how certain the authorities are that
Arnold will live only through his prose. They
pigeonhole the author of *Thyrsis* and *The Forsaken
Merman* as a prosewriter. Even at this time certain
rebels objected: "Did not Arnold write poetry?" As
if in answer, the *North British Review* stated
definitely in March, 1865: "It is Mr. Arnold's prose
writings which will gain for him the greatest and
most enduring reputation."

If Arnold was known, about the year 1865, as a
writer of prose, it is, nevertheless, clear that even
at this time his poetry was quietly winning respect.
An American edition had appeared in 1856, and in
January, 1863, the *North American Review* notes
that although Arnold's poetry "has been six years
before the American public without attracting extensive notice," it is now known to the few. This was
true not only of America, but of England. The
habitués of Parnassus began to discuss this new
poetry. Browning urges Arnold to reprint *Empedocles.* Swinburne is desirous of meeting him, and
Rossetti's diary for May 23, 1867, quotes Swinburne
on Arnold: he is "more satisfactory as a poetic writer

than either Browning or Tennyson." (Swinburne
was indeed devoted until he heard, unluckily, that
Arnold had christened him "a pseudo-Shelley"!)

Swinburne, however, eighteen years after the ap-
pearance of Arnold's first poems, published in the
Fortnightly Review an eloquent appreciation of
Arnold's poetic achievement. This criticism is in
Swinburne's most ecstatic manner, but is sincere, and
suggests the quality of Arnold's poetic influence.

"To some boys at Eton," Swinburne writes, *"Sohrab
and Rustum, Tristram and Iseult,* have been close and
common friends, their streams of Oxus and bays of
Brittany familiar almost as the well-loved Thames weirs
and reaches."

The peroration is Swinburnian, but one fact is evident: Swinburne's faith in Arnold's poetic immortality.

"His verse," so the tribute continues, "bathes us with
fresh radiance and light rain, when weary of the violence
of summer and winter in which others dazzle and detain
us; his spring wears here and there a golden waif of
autumn, his autumn a rosy stray of spring. His tones
and efforts are pure, lucid, aërial; he knows by some
fine impulse of temperance all rules of distance, of
reference, of proportion; nothing is thrust or pressed
upon our eyes, driven or beaten into our ears."

And the essay ends: "These are the trophies of his
work and the gifts of his hand; through these and such
as these things, his high and distinct seat is assured him
among English poets."

Swinburne was, in some ways, the friend of the obscure or the misjudged poet. His praise, notwithstanding, presaged the growing respect for Arnold's poetry among cultivated men and women of the 'seventies and 'eighties. From this time forward, it had, as a contemporary critic said, "a gradual emergence." Incidentally, Arnold had to regain favour with many whom he had alienated by his prose mannerisms. "It sets my teeth on edge . . ." Leslie Stephen wrote Charles Eliot Norton, speaking of Arnold's jaunty air; but he added immediately: "I seriously hold him to be a very good poet." This conviction of Stephen's found a fuller expression in the delightful appraisal, *Matthew Arnold,* in the second volume of *Studies of a Biographer.* Mrs. Browning had written praises from Italy in 1849, and Henry James declared his faith in Arnold's poetry. Meanwhile "the few" in America became more numerous and more enthusiastic. George Woodberry stated that Arnold's poetry seemed more important and more permanent than his prose, and the *Century* for April, 1882, spoke of it as "by far his most important and most permanent contribution to literature."

Thus, when Arnold died twelve years before the end of the century, his poetry had already reached the fit audience though few, if it had not indeed done more than that. Moreover, Arnold was so well known as an original figure in literary and social criticism that many readers turned to his poetry out of curiosity. Perhaps there was about 1890 a natural

84

reaction towards the poetry. Stead got out a penny edition of it, and it was certainly more widely read than in the preceding decade. Critics began to write solemnly on the relative importance of the prose and the poetry. Pedestrian individuals studied it, and proclaimed that they had discovered Arnold's "message." He came to be mentioned with Tennyson and Browning still more frequently, though usually with the warning that Arnold could never be as popular as they. The *Athenæum* of April 4, 1888, reminded its readers that Arnold "began life as a poet, and in a measure remained one always"; and the *Nation,* during the same year, while admitting that *Culture and Anarchy* and *Literature and Dogma* were familiar to thousands who had never read his poems, declared flatly: "It is as a poet if at all that he achieved enduring fame."

More and more, it is evident, the noble seriousness of Arnold's poetry affected the thoughtful readers of the latter part of the century. The calm voices of *Mycerinus,* of *Empedocles,* became slowly a part of the nation's poetic consciousness. Writers so different as Augustine Birrell, W. E. Henley, and Austin Dobson acknowledged its strength, and we find many men speaking of the consoling power of the poetry of Matthew Arnold. Had Arnold lived, he might have thought all this a fulfilment of his prophecy. His faith in his portrayal of the movement of mind would have seemed justified. The most reflecting men of the time found something in Arnold which was lacking in the earlier nineteenth-century poets, or even in Tennyson or Browning. Certain reviews even suggested that Arnold's poetry had popularity. The *Spectator* of March 25, 1893, said that

> "Matthew Arnold can hardly be called a popular poet, yet he is a poet probably more especially popular with the literary class than any other poet of our day."

As if in confirmation Macmillan issued, in this very year, the thirtieth reprint of Arnold's *Selected Poems*. "Favourite passages" from Arnold—a fair evidence of popularity—had vogue. Through Stead's penny edition the more didactic poems attained a considerable circulation. Although allowance must be made for booksellers' puffery, Stead's account of the reception of his edition merits attention:

> "From all parts of the land," he writes, "I have received the most cordial letters from readers who learnt for the first time the charm of Matthew Arnold's verse. . . . Ministers were surprised to find working men, to whom they were paying a pastoral visit, full of interest in Matthew Arnold."

All of which, written in 1896, is rather ridiculous. The chances are that most working-men drank their beer, and paid no homage to Matthew Arnold. The judgment of H. D. Traill made about the same time is more convincing:

> "I do not find any very convincing ground for the belief that the taste of any great multitudes of men in

this or any other country will ever be powerfully attracted by poetry like that of Mr. Arnold."

Stead's letters, however, show the direction of the wind. Arnold's poetry had reached a wider group of readers than that of the intellectuals. Many men were reading, in the twelve years following Arnold's death, not the prose, but *Thyrsis, The Forsaken Merman,* and the other lyrics.

Well, Matthew Arnold has been dead thirty-four years. Most of the men who knew him intimately are also gone. The critics and friends have fired their fusillades of diaries, recollections, and *post mortem* reminiscences. Inevitably, value has become the test of Arnold's poetry. What survives? Once more, who reads Matthew Arnold's poetry?

When a twentieth-century publisher was asked this question he opened his bill of sales under Arnold. One feels, like Chesterton when he heard a writer intimate to what heights can rise "a Shakespeare, a Burns, and an Ingersoll": an impulse to run and whisper such a delightful incident to Arnold's tomb in Laleham Churchyard. Yet, after all, this was a reasonable test. To read an author's book is a compliment; to buy it a recognition. And we can test in some measure the influence of Arnold's prose and poetry upon our generation by the history of their sales. It would be interesting to examine somewhat patiently such a history, if we could construct it, from about the year 1880 until the present day.

It is probable that before 1880 few people spent a shilling on the poetry of Arnold; and 1880 was more than thirty years after the publication of the first volume. A second edition of the *New Poems* appeared in 1868, but the *Selected Poems,* which was more popular, was not printed until 1878. In contrast with this faint response to the poetry, it is noteworthy that at this time *St. Paul and Protestantism* had passed through its third edition; *Essays in Criticism,* also its third; and *Literature and Dogma,* its fifth. And such records take no account of the popularity of other prose works, notably *Culture and Anarchy.*

But during the next twenty years, the balance shifted from the prose to the poetry, slowly, but decisively. In the 'eighties the sale of the prose works continued, almost unabated, but reprints of the poems, especially of the early verses, sonnets, and elegiacs, crept into the libraries of English and American homes. During the 'nineties no less than fifteen reprints of Arnold's poetry made their appearance either in collected works or in anthology form. In the same period only a half-dozen of the prose texts were republished. These were, of course, more available, because of their large circulation in the past, but, even so, the absence of demand for reprints is significant. Records of this sort, though, of course, not conclusive evidence, are suggestive. After 1900 the demand for reprints of the prose was still less. It seems clear that the popularity of the prose had lessened. This might have been foretold: the issues of the prose were ephemeral. Nevertheless, the fact should be noticed. *Essays in Criticism* is still widely read, but the other prose, so admired twenty years earlier, such as *St. Paul and Protestantism, God and the Bible,* or even *Culture and Anarchy,* has suffered a diminuendo.

On the other hand, during the years since 1880, Arnold's poetry found its way into innumerable popular series and was re-edited and re-introduced by such critics as Richard Garnett and A. T. Quiller-Couch. Again one feels that longing to hasten to Laleham and confide to the poet that he may now be read in *Broadway Booklets* and *Roses of Parnassus!* In 1913 there were purchasable in England only two different editions of the *Essays;* three of the *Essays in Criticism;* and one of *Literature and Dogma.* Aside from the essay *On Translating Homer,* of which two editions were procurable, the devotee of Arnold's prose was forced to order the collected works. Opposed to this dearth, seven different editions of the *Poems* could be obtained, besides two of the *Narrative Poems;* five of the *Selections;* three of the *Scholar-Gipsy,* with or without *Thyrsis;* four of *Sohrab and Rustum;* one each of *The Forsaken Merman, Tristram and Iseult,* and— strange resurrection!—*Merope.* Since 1913 the tendency to republish the poems rather than the prose has not appreciably altered.

In America the "gradual emergence" of Arnold's poetry has been equally definite, though naturally the contrast between the prose and poetry was less marked here. The popularity of Arnold's prose was never so great in America as in England, for

America, even if concentrated Philistinism, refused steadily to take "sweetness and light" seriously. The prose works were on sale, but it was enough for the Americans, as General Grant said, to hear the British lion roar. In 1899 there were available eight different editions of Arnold's poetical works, and only one of his prose. *Sweetness and Light,* much distilled, was to be had on India paper between the coloured bindings of a decorative parlor format.

An eccentric phase of Matthew Arnold's poetic fame in America has been the use of selected poems in elementary and secondary schools. A ten-cent version of *Self-Dependence* is the most startling; *Thyrsis* and the *Scholar-Gipsy* are the most absurd of these attempts to commit Arnold's poetry to the innocents. If we stop children on their way to school, we may sometimes see, tucked in between an algebra and a geography, a copy of *Sohrab and Rustum*—an imposing book, with annotations, a biography, and a terrifying chromo of the author. During the last twenty years there have been almost annual editions of *Sohrab and Rustum,* and of the other narrative poems. In college Arnold's poetry is read, on the whole more frequently than his prose, and although university librarians will tell you that there is not excessive demand for either, in general Arnold's poetry receives preference over his prose. In America, then, if we compare the complete prose with the complete poetry, it may be said that Arnold's influence is exerted mainly through the medium of his poetry.

The Poetical Reputation

If I am right, then, in concluding that Arnold's influence, both in England and in America, since his death has resided in his poetry rather than in his prose, it should be remarked in passing how few are the poems on which this influence rests. Posterity is capricious about what it remembers. We have almost forgotten Arnold's ambitious attempts in poetry. *Merope* is for scholars, and *Empedocles,* except for its lyrics, is a curiosity. The college student, the lover of English poetry, the browser in literature are moved to admiration by a half-dozen lovely lyrics. "Tell Mat," said Tennyson, "not to write any more of those prose things like *Literature and Dogma* but to give us something like his *Thyrsis,* or *The Forsaken Merman."* Possibly *The Forsaken Merman* has been more admired than any other single poem of Arnold's. Swinburne's worship of this poem is the voice of the world.

Unquestionably, Arnold's poetry has a hold on the literary men of the present. Mr. H. G. Wells thinks that only industrious students read Matthew Arnold's poetry: "His influence upon religious affairs was profound, but it has sunken in and is not credited to him very much." Possibly this is true; Arnold's influence may be greater in religion than in poetry. But others disagree. Perhaps we may disregard those poets of our day who, to quote a modern novelist, "utterly reject anything more recent than Homer and Sappho and haven't much to say for them." "They," he adds, "would certainly be most scornful of Arnold as they are even of Keats and Shelley."

91

But Mr. Masefield writes: "I should say that all who care for English poetry read Matthew Arnold's *Thyrsis,* "*Scholar-Gipsy*," *Strayed Reveller,* "*Dover Beach*," or the lyrics in *Empedocles*." And Mr. Hugh Walpole, after referring to the influence of the *Scholar-Gipsy,* notes the existence of a group of poets who "are most certainly influenced by Arnold," namely Squire, Freeman, Drinkwater, Shanks, Turner, Nichols: *"They read him and quote him."*

There is a basis, then, for the belief that Matthew Arnold's poetry is still a living force. To many it will always seem remote. "Too cold for me," a lover of poetry once remarked. Yet I—though this is but the witnessing of one—repeatedly discover men and women who are fond of Arnold's poetry. They say little of this. How can you describe what Arnold does for you? Yet faith in his poetry does exist. "I think," Mr. Henry Nevinson says, "his influence is increasing." And Mr. Noyes compares Arnold's lyrics to certain poems of Tennyson's, in respect to their enduring qualities:

> "I believe that the best poetry of Tennyson (such a poem as *In Memoriam*) will always have a great influence on a certain quiet section of the public—the section that happens to make the opinion of posterity! . . . The same applies to the poetry of Matthew Arnold."

Those who seek emotional peace will not turn to Arnold. He is for the unflinching, and, perhaps, only for the strong. But he is honest, and he never offers second-best. Above all, he can, in things of

92

the spirit, lead from darkness to reasonable light. George Eliot once confessed that of all modern poetry Arnold's was most steadily *growing* upon her. Her experience is shared by many readers of poetry.

"It is to him and Clough," says George Woodberry, "that the men of the future will come who desire to find the clearest expression of the most cultivated and thoughtful men of our generation."

Matthew Arnold and His Contemporaries

Matthew Arnold and His Contemporaries

THE centenary of Matthew Arnold in 1922 reminded us that there is yet no adequate life of the
poet-critic. Possibly the importance of Arnold's
social criticism has faded, but his literary criticism
and his poetry are still significant, and are likely to
remain so. In the present revaluation of the Victorians a life of Matthew Arnold might do much.
Such a book would make a great deal of those canons
of judgment which were at first received as capricious
conclusions and which are now accepted as premises
in nineteenth-century criticism: that Dryden and
Pope are "classics of our prose"; that we incline too
much to a "personal estimate" of Shelley; that "the
poetical performance of Wordsworth is, after that
of Shakespeare and Milton, . . . undoubtedly the
most considerable in our language from the Elizabethan age to the present time."

Certainly this biography should point out Arnold's
attitude towards other Victorian poets and critics.
No one has ever aired this peculiarity of Arnold's.
It is assumed that Arnold spoke as frankly about
Tennyson, of whom he was jealous, as about Emerson, of whom he was fond. (The comments on
America which leaked out after Arnold's journey
here in 1883 are supposed to be typical of his frank-
ness towards his fellow-poets. We asked him what
he thought of us. He told us—and we are still
irritated.) Exactly a week ago an American told me
sentimentally that he could not bear to go to Lale-

ham Churchyard after reading the *Letters;* and only yesterday another discoursed on Arnold's "conceited speeches" in the United States.

Of all literary junkets to our country the echoes of this journey have reverberated furthest. When Arnold arrived in America, Main Street had just been laid out, and the expert on the Philistine walked down it with an observant eye. "The Matthew Arnold *troupe*," read the passport given the lecturer in New York. And Mr. Barnum, I have heard, had already written: "You are a celebrity; I am a notoriety; we ought to get together." Chicago, too, was genial. One newspaper, reporting his lecture there, bore the caption: "Matthew Has Whiskers!" True or not, the legend still flourishes that when Arnold demurred, humbly, as became "a being of dim faculties and bounded knowledge," that Chicago seemed to him to lack culture, a defender replied: "Well, Chicago ain't took up culture yet, but when she does she'll certainly make it hum." The poet is said to have admitted that perhaps Denver and the Far West were not yet ripe for Mr. Matthew Arnold.

Arnold did not make culture hum here. Let that be conceded. But he spoke without reserve of American customs and American literature. He thought we were Philistines, and when assailed by the well-known question—need it be phrased?—he said: we were just that—Philistines. But the inference that he sniffed openly at his British contemporaries does not follow. What a study of the

Matthew Arnold and His Contemporaries

Essays in Criticism proves is his silence on this very point. Poets of the earlier generation he scolded; he remarked also the faults of Gray, Milton, and Shakespeare. But we look in vain in his essays for criticisms of the poetry of Tennyson, of Browning, or of Swinburne.

Nevertheless, concerning all these Matthew Arnold had his opinions. The natural theory that the professor of poetry, the champion of the literature of the past, cared first of all for the proven body of English literature is insufficient. He decried the "caprice" of contemporary literature; "hot, dizzy trash," he called it. Yet he watched the passing pageant of poetry and fiction carefully. He read eagerly the poems of Tennyson as they came from the press. More than this, he had his ear to the ground, so that he sometimes knew the plans of the Laureate, as in the writing of *Lucretius*. Browning advised him about *Empedocles*. He took counsel of Swinburne concerning *The New Sirens*. He followed the work of these two poets, and of many others, with an intense interest.

His silence did not come from indifference. It came from the conflict in his mind of disapproval and tact. He was urged to speak out about Americans—and he yielded. Concerning his English contemporaries he never spoke out. Spreading opinions, honest but unpleasant—this was a luxury which Arnold, like most of us, could not afford. His attitude is made clear in a letter to Lady de Rothschild, written on September 25, 1864. He said:

"I have been very much pressed to write a criticism on Tennyson, *apropos* of his new volume; but is this possible to be done with the requisite freedom by any one who has published verses himself? I mean, for instance, I do not think Tennyson a *grand et puissant esprit,* and therefore I do not really set much store by him, in spite of his popularity; but is it possible for me to say this? I think not."

Most readers of Victorian literature are sorry that Arnold thought not. Who would not like *Essays in Criticism* to include, in the manner of the Wordsworth essay, discussions of Tennyson, Swinburne, and Browning? So many of the reviews of these poets were interesting only as critical antics. A volume of critical essays like George Brimley's with Matthew Arnold's name on the title-page would be altogether desirable; but such a volume was never written. The English disciple of Sainte-Beuve left no word on the poets and prose writers of his own age.

No formal word. But Matthew Arnold's informal judgments on his contemporaries are many; there are allusions, phrases, comments—everywhere. Compared to a book of essays they are microscopic, but they have immense interest if we are at all retrospective about the Victorians. And we are; these are the decades of Victorian centenaries. In 1860 Arnold remarked to his sister that he meant to "say boldly the truth about a great many English celebrities." He did it boldly,—as one writes a diary boldly. Arnold's opinions of his coevals are tucked away in letters to his family, in chance remarks, and in irrelevant prefaces. If these bones are exhumed and fitted together they form a skeleton of literary criticism. And in private judgments of men of letters Arnold, "the elegant Jeremiah," is less elegant, and very candid.*

"The real truth is," he wrote, just after the appearance of the *Idylls of the King,* "that Tennyson, with all his temperament and artistic skill, is deficient in intellectual power." Here is something for Mr. Noyes and the other Tennysonians to meditate upon. Their leader is not artificial, nor supersweet, nor "Victorian." At least these foibles are not the real charges against him. The Laureate merely lacks brains. Two years later Arnold wrote his mother that Tennyson's lines on the Prince Consort did not have "poetical value." He added:

> "They are, as you say, very just, but so was one of the *Times* leaders about the same subject, and above the merit of just remark and proper feeling these lines do not appear to me to rise; but to arrive at the merit of *poetical beauty* you must rise a long way above these."

And in the same year Arnold speaks of "the ridiculous elevation of [Tennyson] above Words-

---

*Besides the opinions on writers the *Letters* contain many interesting references to contemporaries in other fields. Among the judgments on men of his time in a collection made by Professor Dowden are: Froude has "very sinister ways of looking at history"; Disraeli, in his speeches, is given to "heavy pompous pounding"; or, Lord Salisbury is a "dangerous man, chiefly from want of any fine sense and experience of literature and its beneficent functions."

worth." He repeats that he cannot think "Tennyson a great and powerful spirit in any line. . . . My conviction that he will not finally stand high is firm."

Possibly such bluntness was not free from personal feeling. "I am rather troubled," this in 1866, "to find that Tennyson is at work on a subject, the story of the Latin poet Lucretius, which I have been occupied with for some twenty years." Tennyson had committed one sin which even the temperate Arnold found annoying: his poetry was popular, tremendously so. Arnold's was not. La Rochefoucauld's sly maxim may be adapted: "There is something in the adversity of a poet's rivals which is not altogether unpleasing." There was little adversity in Tennyson's later career to please a rival. Arnold, in spite of risky experiments in theories of poetry such as *Sohrab and Rustum* and *Merope,* had an eye to his own reputation as a poet. There is a pithy passage in the *Letters* already quoted in another connection:

> "It might be fairly urged that I have less poetical sentiment than Tennyson, and less intellectual vigor and abundance than Browning; yet, because I have perhaps more of a fusion of the two than either of them, and have more regularly applied that fusion to the main line of modern development, I am likely enough to have my turn, as they have had theirs."

There you have it: Arnold had ambitions, but Tennyson seemed to have, at least in his own day, the fulfilment.

Yet these may be fancies. All that Arnold said of Tennyson squares, it must be acknowledged, with his dogmatic statements concerning poetry. He was likely to deny intellectual power to all poets a shade below Dante and Shakespeare, and to all poetry inferior to the *Iliad* or *Œdipus*. "High seriousness," "interpretative power," "natural magic," "moral profundity"—in these laws Arnold had his poetic being. Literally so. He tried in his own poetry to scale this Olympus. And he applied his tests mercilessly to the poetry of others. Even Mr. Noyes will not say that Tennyson's poetry can survive them.

Arnold found no compensation in the harmonies of Tennyson's verse; he wrote little of metrical technique, although I suspect that he was more interested in it than is generally supposed. We shall not expect then that Swinburne's music will prevent an intellectual verdict from Arnold on "the youngest singer." Arnold measured Swinburne, of course, by the same standards. Aside from worship of Greek literature and a general love of truth, it is difficult to imagine what Arnold and Swinburne had in common. It is amusing merely to picture them together at dinner, as they sometimes were in the 'sixties. Swinburne liked Arnold. In 1867 he reviewed the *New Poems*, praising extravagantly: they were "hyperborean" and "empyrean," and generally, one concludes, made of star-dust.

Moreover, Arnold came to like Swinburne. In various parts of the *Letters* he speaks kindly of him, and on one occasion he pays him a real compliment:

103

at Swinburne's suggestion he alters *The New Sirens.*
All this is very well, but somehow we believe that if
the *Essays in Criticism* had included a paper on Swinburne, the central idea, though softened, would have
been Arnold's first comment on our dancing, quoting,
red-haired little poet. It is to this remark that we
turn with amusement and thoughtfulness: Arnold's
natural reaction to Swinburne. On June 16, 1863,
he wrote his mother:

> "Sunday night I dined with Monckton Milnes, and
> met all the advanced liberals in religion and politics, and
> a Cingalese in full costume. . . . The philosophers were
> fearful! G. Lewes, Herbert Spencer, and"—note
> well!—*"a sort of pseudo-Shelley called Swinburne."*

Another beautiful and ineffectual angel? There can
be no doubt of it. If Arnold had written a critical
essay on Swinburne he would have rated him low—a
little lower, we might say, than the angel.

Multum in parvo. A little acid is as effective
sometimes as a train of dynamite. These single,
sharp comments from the "priest of the kid-glove
persuasion" (with the gloves off!) damn as decisively
as a twenty-page review. Hear them. Alexander
Smith is "a phenomenon of a very dubious character." Charlotte Brontë's mind "contains nothing
but hunger, rebellion, and rage." Henry Crabb
Robinson's *Diary* has much in it that is "twaddling."
Although Arnold likes parts of Lowell's discourse at
Birmingham, he feels "the want of body and current
in the discourse as a whole." And so on. An in-

spection of the estate of Bulwer Lytton produced the
following:

> "Like Lord Lytton himself, the place is a strange
> mixture of what is really romantic and interesting with
> what is tawdry and gim-cracky."

The relaxed tone of these private judgments ex-
tends to brief judgments on writers of the past.
Arnold has tossed away the urbanity of his formal
essays. In the essay on Shelley occurred the famous
euphemism: Shelley was "a beautiful and ineffectual
angel." But in the *Letters* Shelley is, flatly, "as incoherent as the darkness itself." In *The Study of
Poetry* Burns ". . . comes short of the high seriousness of the great classics"; his world is "a world of
Scotch drink, Scotch religion, and Scotch manners."
But in the *Letters* Arnold is more definitive. Burns
is this: "a beast with splendid gleams."

It is, however, unfair to think that the phrases are
always adverse. Arnold likes Margaret Fuller; he
admires Bulwer; and, though he prefers Hesiod,
Kingsley's *Hypatia* is "vigorous and interesting."
He has even a taste for Jean Ingelow, Harriet Mar-
tineau, and Miss Mitford! Nevertheless, the impression remains that the world is crammed with bad
writers. Thackeray's death is sad, but not for literature, for Thackeray is not a great writer. Such
statements are amazing, not merely because they are
tart, but because they are sincere. Even the social
gadflies, the opponents of Philistinism in other quar-
ters, have only a half-hearted sympathy from Arnold.

His tributes to Carlyle are numerous, and in the essay on Emerson profoundly moving. Nevertheless, his sharp dig at Carlyle in the *Letters* probably represents his real opinion. Writing to M. Fontanès in 1881 Arnold says: "I never much liked Carlyle. He seemed to me 'carrying coals to Newcastle,' as our proverb says; preaching earnestness to a nation which had plenty of it by nature." Ruskin, an unacknowledged ally in "sweetness and light," he could not endure: "The man and character too febrile, irritable, and weak to possess the *ordo concatenatioque veri.*" Must we all have Greek balance and measure? Apparently—and luckily—Ruskin did not conform; he did not have "high seriousness," "totality of impression," and the other Hellenic virtues. At the dinner which stamped Swinburne as a pseudo-Shelley Arnold met and talked with Ruskin. "I should never," he declares, "like him." Later he added, as a summary of Ruskin, that it was his custom to be "dogmatic and *wrong.*"

The significant deduction from all this is not that Arnold liked nobody and nobody's poetry. He did like a few poets and a few poems of his own day. Browning and Clough seem to have pleased him. He liked Browning's themes from the Greek, and he listened to him regarding *Empedocles*. (Incidentally, his favour did not include Mrs. Browning. He made brief disposition of this lady in a letter to Madame du Quaire in 1858: "As to his wife," Arnold says in respect to Browning, "I regard her as hopelessly confirmed in her aberration from health, nature, beauty, and truth.") His belief in Clough is well known, they two agreeing, as Arnold said, "like two lambs in a world of wolves." Arnold's affection for Clough is understandable; his faith in him as the arbiter of literature is, today, inexplicable. It was, I suppose, kinship of spirit. "You and Clough are, I believe," he wrote Mrs. Forster, "the two people I in my heart care most to please by what I write." And at Clough's death occurs this astounding tribute: "He is one of the few people who ever made a deep impression upon me."

It is, of course, important, and very interesting, that so remarkable a critic of literature as Arnold should have failed completely in evaluating his contemporaries. Fortunate is it, on second thought, at least for his own reputation, that he did not publish other critical essays in which he enlarged these mistaken convictions. One blunder like the Shelley essay is quite enough. It would be difficult to assemble from the writings of any other first-rate nineteenth-century critic guesses about posthumous fame more unlucky than these. Is this the result of concentration upon the literature of the past? No, I fancy that this weakness is temperamental; that is, inexplicable. One beholds often the spectacle of distinguished men of letters prophesying absurdly, even as Arnold did of Tennyson; while obscure reviewers may divine the truth. Walter Savage Landor's opinions of his contemporaries were foolish—observe his adoration of Southey—yet so humble a person as George Brimley saw clearly the enduring qualities in Shelley, Wordsworth, or Thackeray. Arnold's blind spot for the poetry of Mrs. Browning or his adulation of Clough are no more mysterious than his singular misunderstanding of fiction. Imagine his believing that Thackeray was not a power in literature! The great critics who can judge wisely of the present, as well as the past, like the uncanny Hazlitt, are indeed few. We must take Arnold as he was: one defect in him as a critic was his inability to estimate properly his contemporaries.

But the significant deduction is rather this, that Arnold was true to his ideals in poetry. "The best that is known and thought in the world" was a happy phrase, but to him it was more than a phrase; it was a creed. His touchstones for poetry, seemingly so flexible, were in reality like steel. A single line of Dante exposed, he thought, the glitter of Tennyson. He thought it unwise to speak out in formal essays concerning his contemporaries, but the sharp phrases found in the *Letters* may, in every case, be traced to Arnold's principles of poetry as he continued to see them until the end of his life. Arnold praised the ancients, but, unlike some of his brother poets, he read and studied them as well. He depended upon no contemporary poet for inspiration, unless it were Wordsworth, and such enthusiasms as Browning felt for Landor, or Swinburne for Rossetti, were unknown to him. His intimacies and his communion were with the past which endures. Compared with this, the present was as the fashion of this world which passeth away.

Three Aspects of Matthew Arnold's Poetry

Three Aspects of Matthew Arnold's Poetry

A LOVER of Matthew Arnold's poetry who was a persistent student of his poetic methods once said in my hearing that Arnold's verse possessed three characteristics which made it unique in nineteenth-century poetry. These three, the devotee declared, are recurrent; and though not everywhere apparent, they are Arnold's predominant traits as a Victorian poet. It is not wise to be dogmatic about qualities of poetry, and few of us would limit Arnold's to three, but such a criticism of Arnold's poetry, however artificial, merits consideration. The three characteristics are: a mastery of mood-creating detail; a sacrifice of narrative to philosophical ideas; and a very special type of Hellenism.

We can sometimes discern the essence of a writer's thought in his minor poems. In the poetic novitiate, before the *ars celare artem* has appeared, we may detect clearly the poet's most instinctive aims. It may seem unfair to test by apprentice work, but in this ideas and themes are often remarkably distinct, unconfused by elaboration. To appreciate the complex structure of the oriole's nest, we must watch him at the first of his weaving. To understand the perfection of Tennyson's *Lady of Shalott* we must examine some of the bad first stanzas of this poem. Matthew Arnold has written four poems, which, besides being very early in time of composition, fall, when considered in relation to his longer works, into

the place of minor poems. The four poems pro-
claim unaffectedly these three characteristics.

For mood-creating detail, there is *The Forsaken
Merman.* The poem has an obscure story, is lyrical
in tone, and in its suggestion of loneliness may possibly allude dimly to Arnold's own experience in
nineteenth-century thought. Like the merman, Arnold
cannot, because of something in his nature and manner of thinking, worship in the Church, as do the
others. He can only look on, somewhat unhappily,
as the merman watches Margaret. But the charm
of *The Forsaken Merman* for most readers—and
few poems of Arnold's have a wider audience—depends upon its delicate and haunting pictures; on its
subtle moods of feeling, half human, half unearthly.

Many students of Arnold's poetry have been
curious, at one time or another, about the history of
this poem: the reason for Arnold's interest in the
theme and the source of the legend. Did Arnold,
for instance, know Fouqué's *Undine?* Had he been
browsing about in folk-lore of the northern peoples,
as he did in that of the Celts? There is no biography
of Arnold which can tell us. It seems probable that
about the time of the composition of *The Forsaken
Merman* he was reading widely in German literature,
but this hypothesis does not aid us greatly. We do
know that he was familiar with the ghostly traditions
of the North Coast. He wrote of the Neckan, Saint
Brandan, and the Merman. He must have known
something of cognate legends: sirens who bewitch
fishing fleets; merbabies who are washed ashore and

are buried by landsmen of the northern shores. He may have known the ballad of *Die Schöne Agniese*.

Or, we should like to believe, he knew and liked the Danish ballad on the same theme, not probably in the original, but in George Borrow's version. This poem is startlingly like *The Forsaken Merman*. There is, of course, no actual proof that this old tale was the original of Arnold's poem. Its mood is severe; that of *The Forsaken Merman* is plaintive. Moreover, the conclusion is different. Yet it is possible that Arnold studied these very lines:

> The Merman up to the church door came;
> His eyes they shone like a yellow flame;
>
> His face was white, and his beard was green—
> A fairer demon was never seen.
>
> "Now, Agnes, Agnes, list to me,
> Thy babes are longing so after thee."
>
> "I cannot come yet, here must I stay
> Until the priest shall have said his say."
>
> And when the priest had said his say,
> She thought with her mother at home she'd stay.

Although no one can assert positively, this poem is rather like the buried ancestor of Arnold's poem revisiting the upper air.

Such speculations indicate, in any case, the elaboration of Arnold's version of the legend. Out of the

rude elements of the old story Arnold has chiselled
a delicate cameo. Every detail contributes to the
mood of strange melancholy. Various critics have
observed how Arnold dwells upon the wind. Coming
from the still places far beneath the ocean surface
the Merman cannot endure the fresh breezes which
blow across the shore, and which have long been part
of Margaret's mortal life. So the forsaken husband
comes to his wife only in moments of calm; and when
the great winds shoreward blow, he longs to flee back
to his windless home in the deep sea. He hates the
village church, for it is on the windy hill, and as he
peers into it, looking for Margaret, he shrinks before the cold, blowing airs. If Margaret will not
return to him, her punishment is to be the loss of
husband and children, but, hardly less, she will also
forfeit:

> Sand-strewn caverns, cool and deep,
> Where the winds are all asleep.

The Merman would have her tortured by the sound
of winds, and by the gusty shaking of the doors!

There is charm in all this, and in the fancy which
creates for us the Merman's home among the sand-
strewn caverns. Through legends, through pictures,
and through actual sight of deep sea flowers, we have
all sometime made for ourselves strange romances
of the unplumbed depths of the ocean. We recall,
perhaps, *Die Versunkene Glocke.* And an American
poet sings:

> The water is calm and still below,
> For the winds and waves are absent there,
> And the sands are bright as the stars that glow
> In the motionless fields of open air:
> There, with its waving blade of green,
> The sea-flag streams through the silent water
> And the crimson leaf of the dulse is seen
> To blush, like a banner bathed in slaughter:
> There, with light and easy motion,
> The fan-coral sweeps through the clear, deep sea;
> And the yellow and scarlet tufts of ocean
> Are bending like corn on the upland lea.

So Arnold's poem is touched with the magic of life in the sea-deeps; we dream, almost believing, of the mysterious life of sea-beasts, of marine flowers, of the quiver and gleam of spent lights. Arnold stirs the imagination by occult sights and sounds. Red-gold thrones shine faintly, and through the secret, windless abysses is intoned the tintinnabulation of a ghostly bell. All this is definite, yet mystical—boons for the inner eye and ear.

The mood of strangeness is accentuated in other ways, among them that of the refrain. Apart from its lingering cadences we feel the Merman's insistence on the line, as has been often noted:

> Children dear, was it *yesterday?*

He is insensible, apparently, in his life in the sea, to the passage of time. The point is insignificant, but it adds subtly to the total impression, that of un-human regret and longing. We seem to see the

white-walled town, the church on the windy hill, and
the Merman looking through the window. Inside
sits Margaret, her eyes fixed on the holy book.
Arnold tells us nothing definite. It is a picture, and
we must interpret for ourselves its wistful beauty.

Arnold's tendency to stress a philosophical idea at
the expense of narrative or dramatic effects may be
observed in many poems, among them that on Empedocles,—which Arnold himself repudiated. But
he does this sort of thing also in two poems, *Mycerinus* and *The Sick King in Bokhara*. In some
respects these are complementary, almost interde-
pendent; they may always be studied profitably together. In each story the central figure is a king,
youthful in years and in attitude towards life. *The
Sick King in Bokhara* is Asian in theme. It is
reminiscent of remote dynasties. Like *Sohrab and
Rustum*, it takes us back to ancient names and places;
we think of Mervè, Orgunjè, and Samarcand. Mycerinus, too, is a king of dim legend. But both poems
are Greek in tone, and the source of the former is
Herodotus.

Mycerinus is stunned by the decree of an oracle
which cuts him off with only six more years of life.
He suffers, however, less from fear of death than
from spiritual confusion. For, although Mycerinus's
father had been evil, he enjoyed long life, whereas
Mycerinus himself, though good, is doomed to die
in early manhood. Mycerinus meditates bitterly on
the overthrow of his notions of justice. For Mycerinus had been orthodox. He had believed that

justice implied reward for good, or, as he says, that man's idea of justice was but a reflection of the compelling justice of the gods. But in the decree of the oracle he finds cogent evidence that the gods have their own fancies about what is "just." Mycerinus feels that his ethics have been askew; and not least in his chagrin is the realization that his virtue, based on his self-conceived idea of justice, has deprived him of joy by the way, of the sense-pleasures of life. In his concentration upon righteousness he has missed a gay youth. Cynically speaking, his has been a wasted life, for, as Renan implies, if there is not justice in heaven, then are the wise lovers of virtue really fools, and the so-called pleasure-lovers the truly wise men. The ideals of Mycerinus have been:

> Vain dreams, which quench our pleasures, then depart,
> When the duped soul, self-master'd, claims its meed;
> When, on the strenuous just man, Heaven bestows,
> Crown of his struggling life, an unjust close!

In the meantime the gulled Mycerinus, worshipping justice which now seems to him a phantom, has missed life itself. He has had:

> . . . no joy in dances crown'd with flowers,
> Love, free to range, and regal banquetings.

He has, in fact, been naïve. He has not noticed the flourishing bay-trees of the wicked, but, as he meditates now, he seems to see nothing else. So he thinks, and, accordingly, he rearranges his philosophy. Pos-

117

sibly, he fancies, even the gods themselves may be constrained, like him; they, too, may not be free, and may be under the sway of some higher destiny than that which he ascribed to them. They, too, may feel the force of what restrains him now, the dire and mysterious Law, hateful 'Ανάγκη, which compelleth both men and gods.

Perhaps so. At any rate Mycerinus does at first the obvious thing. He forces himself to a belated worship of pleasure. He plans to take the remaining six years at the full. We find him in his palm-grove:

> . . . holding high feast, at morn,
> Rose-crown'd.

He devotes the six years to pleasure. Possibly this is all. One must not read too much into those last stanzas of the poem. It is possible to conceive of Mycerinus as a conventional free-liver, but this is not, I believe, Arnold's meaning. Mycerinus does not make either a good Stoic or an Epicurean. Perhaps it is the influence of past years. But he is yet the lover of virtue. He finds the feast joyless. He still meditates upon his strange destiny. He sees in it all a working out of a Law, and as the years pass, he becomes sensible of its meaning. At the feast he:

> Took measure of his soul, and knew its strength,
> And by that silent knowledge, day by day,
> Was calm'd, ennobled, comforted, sustain'd.

Mycerinus learned to submit to the Law.

118

The experience of the King in Bokhara is somewhat similar. As he rides forth secure, indifferent, a prostrate man bars his way, begging judgment by law. In a drought of the country he has kept drink from his mother and cursed her. Conscience-stricken he now seeks atonement. The King is not unkind but brushes him aside as a fanatic. But the slave stops him again, importuning him with the same plea. Again the King turns him off. Still a third time the man supplicates the King. Puzzled, but still kind, the King exacts negligently the penalty of the Law, himself casting the first stone. The slave dies, joyful, praising Allah.

For the King this is revelation. He comes to perceive that the slave is not a fanatic, but a human soul desiring to fulfil his conception of law. The contrast of this creature's sense of responsibility—to such law as he knew—with his own nonchalance in judgment makes him meditate on the whole question of the Law which seems to rule men. He sees in the slave a man with a higher conception of the Law than he himself possesses, for the slave had learned that, to attain happiness, he must fulfil the Law. Bokhara buries the slave with the honours of a King, and, like Mycerinus, he reflects. He feels that both slave and King are subject to Law, and that the Law must be obeyed. This is in effect the same sense of Law which Mycerinus felt.

The conception of a moral law is a favourite idea in Arnold's poetry. Not only is it a theme which seems to link these two poems, but it finds expression in *Sohrab and Rustum, Balder Dead,* and in many shorter poems. Moreover, to the idea itself and its interpretation Arnold sacrifices a great deal. For what interests a lover of narrative poetry as he reads *Mycerinus* and *The Sick King in Bokhara* is the lack of emphasis upon dramatic situations. Both these poems have marked possibilities as dramatic poems. But, as in *Empedocles on Etna,* Arnold cares only for the idea. The oracle in *Mycerinus,* the slave's sin in *The Sick King in Bokhara* are merely grist for Arnold's purpose,—the development of thought.

The *Strayed Reveller,* the fourth poem, illustrates Arnold's Hellenism. Arnold's love of Greek life and thought permeates all his poetry; it is absurd to think of it as centered in any single poem. Nor does any one poem illustrate the differences between Arnold and other nineteenth-century poets who turn to Greece for inspiration. Yet one special characteristic *The Strayed Reveller* has: it indicates Arnold's independence of spirit in writing of a Greek theme in a Greek manner. That is to say, in this poem he wrote of a traditional Greek theme without a suspicion of what he himself called "Hebraism": the alteration of the story to achieve a moral lesson.

As is often suggested, a poem very like *The Strayed Reveller* in situation is Milton's *Comus.* In both is the tale of the seductions of Circe; in both are the banquet and the magic drugs, even to the hæmony of *Comus* and the wine of *The Strayed Reveller.* But from the first line of the opening stanza Arnold's poem is Greek,—Greek in the

irregular choric metres, in the scene, and in the ideas.
Instead of Miltonic strictness of conscience we re-
joice in the calm and happy gods. Here, too, are the
bards, who with labour and pain attain the vision of
the Olympians. The eternal difference between the
two poems lies in the spirit animating each, a difference especially evident in their conclusions. For Milton's concern is to teach a lesson: Heaven will stoop
to feeble virtue. Arnold does not think of pointing
his poem with a moral. Without apothegms on vir-
ture *The Strayed Reveller* offers us the joy of the
senses:

> Ah, cool night-wind, tremulous stars!
> Ah, glimmering water,
> Fitful earth-murmur.
>
> .   .   .
>
> Faster, faster,
> O Circe, Goddess,
>
> .   .   .   .
>
> The bright procession
> Of eddying forms,
> Sweep through my soul.

It has not been my purpose in this brief study to
analyse these three qualities of Arnold's poetry.
They have been merely mentioned as typical of his
point of view; and the four poems touched on which
constitute the best introduction to these qualities.
Each is an issue which would take us deep into the
essentials of poetry, and into Arnold's theories.
Thus his mastery over mood-creating detail is linked

with his study of poetic expression, discussed in the various *Prefaces* and in the *Essays in Criticism*. His insistence upon the idea in poetry is related to his definition of poetry as "a criticism of life." And the Hellenism found in his poetry is a part of his concept of "spontaneity of consciousness." These characteristics are discussed in the next essay in this volume. We are concerned here with the approach to these characteristics. And the three paths lead, it seems to me, through the four poems named in this essay.

Theory and Practice in the Poetry of
Matthew Arnold

Theory and Practice in the Poetry of Matthew Arnold

"I OWE everything to poetry, for there is no other name to give to the sum total of my thoughts; . . . I owe to it all my consolations in the past; I shall probably owe to it my future." So Maurice de Guérin wrote in his journal, and so, in a sense, Matthew Arnold might have written of himself. The inner life of Arnold is not in his urbane prose so much as in his poetry. We are sure of this not only from Arnold's own poetry, but also from his criticisms of poetry. More than any other nineteenth-century poet, Arnold tried to *define* poetry, just as certain of his contemporaries tried the hardly more difficult task of defining God. Both his prose and verse contain many thoughtful utterances concerning poetry: what it is; what it should be; what it means to him personally. From the essay on *The Literary Influence of Academies* we learn that "poetry is mainly an affair of genius." In the study of *Heinrich Heine* Arnold declares that poetry is "simply the most beautiful, impressive, and widely effective mode of saying things." This, he adds, explains its importance. The conception that poetry is a means of expression, he reconsiders again in speaking of Wordsworth: "Poetry is nothing less than the most perfect speech of man, that in which he comes nearest to being able to utter the truth." Arnold had little interest in æsthetics, but he was continually striving to analyse the essence of the mysterious force that men call poetry.

Not only was Arnold deeply concerned about the nature of poetry, but he aimed to set forth a body of principles which would guide men in its creation. His ideas developed slowly, and, as he read and wrote, changed,—or strengthened into convictions. Perhaps Arnold would have been amused, if he had been told that a considerable *organon* of poetic theory could be formed from his writings. Yet this is so. These theories are scattered, and they have never been collected. They are imbedded in literary criticism, in poetry, even in social criticism. Then, too, they are incomplete. Arnold never replied fully to the attacks on the *Preface of 1853;* and in the *Preface of 1854* he admits what every student of Arnold's poetic theories feels: that the relation of these theories to lyric poetry and other types of poetry he left undetermined. But such a group of principles does exist.

When we have pieced the theories together into some sort of garment, we are aware that it is still far from being a perfect mantle of poetic theory. There are many kinds of poetry which it will not fit at all; it is torn and re-sewn; and it is curiously embroidered with Arnold's own special brocade, as in the case of his unique theory of a "touchstone" method for poetry. We have, after all, only fragments of a theory. But these fragments have unusual interest. Arnold's ideals for poetry are austere. They exclude, undoubtedly, much that is good in poetry. Yet as a whole they exercise a sound influence in the world of poets. They make no compromise with the sins in poetry which Arnold thought unpardonable: triviality, caprice, or emotionalism for its own sake. And they are impatient of the weak, the shallow, or the ephemeral. The main body of Arnold's poetic theories may be found in the *Prefaces,* and in the three series of *Essays in Criticism.* It is necessary to sift them from much extraneous matter, but there they are in all their wealth of suggestion; and they are illumined by many comments, accessible chiefly in the *Mixed Essays* and in the meditative portions of the *Letters.*

Arnold's poetic theory owes much to thinkers of the past, but most of all it is indebted to Aristotle, to Goethe, and to Wordsworth. The theory has value in itself, but its exceptional interest lies in the fact that Arnold endeavoured to put it into practice. He wrote poems in definite illustration of his beliefs. This was dangerous, but Arnold, though he was not without concern for his poetic reputation, was not afraid to fail. He must have known that *Merope* would fall flat; and in the *Preface of 1853* he acknowledges the weakness of *Empedocles on Etna.* Still he persisted in writing according to his own rules. He is with Dryden, Coleridge, and Wordsworth as a poet who risks exemplifying his notions of poetry. Thus it becomes the student's privilege to test Arnold's theories of poetic art by his own practice.

In such a test the odds must be against any poet,

and, perhaps, especially against Arnold who pitches his ideals high. His poems, we discover, are not wholly consistent illustrations of his theories, but they are not, in this respect, failures. Everyone knows the major charge preferred against poems written to prove a theory. Many have found it easy to say that Arnold's poems lack spontaneity; that they are bookish, academic, self-conscious. Such faults are the inevitable by-products of imitation. Arnold is imitative, and for this reason, he is often conscious in manner. But in a high sense Arnold attains his end. He emerges from the test to which he has submitted himself with distinction: his poetry *has* "high seriousness," "interpretative power," "totality of impression," and other key-qualities which he rates so highly; and it has them in generous measure. Arnold falls short of the ideals he has set himself; it could hardly be otherwise. But his achievement is admirable, and by it he sets new standards for poets who come after him.

Arnold's habit of catch-phrases, such as those just mentioned, makes it difficult to arrange his principles in the logical order of their development. "High seriousness," for example, is repeated again and again, sometimes in connection with the subjects for poetry; sometimes apropos of the "criticism of life" theory; and sometimes as a general precept for all good literature. Is then "high seriousness" a root or a branch of his basic theories? No one can say. Like "sweetness and light" it was a phrase connotative of certain ideals for poetry; ideals which, it would appear, were not always thoroughly analysed by Arnold himself. These phrases appear and re-appear, but usually they are subordinate to the two great theories which will always be remembered as distinctively Arnold's.

Besides these two, Arnold put forward many other theories of poetry. But they are slighter in character, and, in some cases, are merely aspects of the two fundamental conceptions of poetry. These, briefly stated, are: Arnold's conviction concerning the proper subjects for poetry, with its attendant doctrines concerning style; and the assertion that poetry is, primarily, "a criticism of life." The former theory was the earlier of the two. In the *Preface of 1853* Arnold amplifies, with much application to modern literature, the Aristotelian theme that "All depends upon the subject; choose a fitting action, penetrate yourself with the feeling of its situations; this done, everything else will follow." This theory stirred and grew in Arnold's mind throughout his life. We meet with the idea everywhere in his prose. Not many years before his death, he wrote, as part of the same theme:

> "A great poet receives his distinctive character of superiority from his application, under conditions immutably fixed by the laws of poetic beauty and poetic truth, from his application, I say, to his *subject,* whatever it may be, of the ideas 'On man, on nature, and on human life.'"

This concept of "the subject" may be considered as the basis of Arnold's poetical philosophy.

This, then, is the first commandment, if we have ideals in writing poetry: choose a worthy subject.

> "What," Arnold asks, "are the eternal objects of poetry, among all nations, and at all times? They are actions; human actions; possessing an inherent interest in themselves, and which are to be communicated in an interesting manner by the art of the Poet."

This is an early statement of Arnold's creed on this point. At this time it appears elementary, but its beginnings are significant.

> "The poet, then," he says, "has in the first place to select an excellent action; and what actions are the most excellent? Those, certainly, which most powerfully appeal to the great primary human affections: to those elementary feelings which subsist permanently in the race, and which are independent of time."

Such is the theory in its simplest form.

From this statement two subsidiary beliefs concerning poetry follow logically. If we accept the premise that the quality of these human actions is the chief consideration, then the date of the action is of no importance. We may find great subjects both in antiquity and in the living present. To paraphrase Carlyle, the one essential is that the subject *"be great."* Prometheus, Œdipus, or Macbeth are great subjects not because of, but irrespective of, their antiquity. The *Persae* and *Childe Harold* are both inferior subjects despite the fact that the former is ancient and the latter modern. Arnold's theory had its origin in Aristotle, and he himself displays a preference for Greek themes, but the selection of a "great subject" is not therefore in any way limited by age or nationality.

Another belief is concerned with the expression of the great subject. The truly great poet never writes merely for the sake of style. On the contrary, he always subordinates manner to subject. The style is thus made an integral part of the subject, but never consciously; it rather follows as the necessary means of expression for the great subject. Indeed, Arnold goes so far as to say that if the subject is really great, in the hands of the man of genius, a fitting style will follow. Naturally, then, the great artist in subject and style will condemn the modern delight in expression for its own sake, the passion for isolated passages of beauty. Purple passages, imagery, felicitous phrases,—all of these, if sought for themselves alone, betray the inferior strain in a poet. If tried by Arnold's austere ideal, the ordinary poet seems almost a trifler. If we accept this theory without reservation, we must pronounce as second-rate many poets to whom beauty is the first consideration, —among them Keats. For the attainment of beauty for its own sake is unworthy of the first-rate poet. He will rather strive, not for beauty, but for excellence of action. And if he achieves this greatness of subject and subordinate greatness of style, he will have also gained another aspect of this ideal—"totality of impression."

Such, in effect, with many criticisms of Keats, of

Shakespeare, of the modern temper towards the poetry of the past, and with the famous comment upon his own *Empedocles,* was the burden of Arnold's *Preface of 1853.* He had already published two volumes of poetry. This *Preface,* however, was the first pronouncement of the theory which was destined to develop, and to affect so deeply his own poetry. The ideas of the *Preface* became fixed principles; its catchwords expanded into doctrines. Thus in the *Preface to Merope* (1858) Arnold repeats: "No man can do his best with a subject which does not penetrate him." In the *Essays in Criticism,* First Series (1865), we hear of the interest of the De Guérins in "great subjects"; in the Second Series (1888) we learn that Wordsworth and Byron excel because they have "truth of substance"; and even Dante and Homer are remarkable mainly for this very reason. By "truth of substance" Arnold meant little else than the "great subject," the type of subject connected with the unchanging moral ideas and passions of the human soul.

To this theory of the importance of subject and action many objections may be raised. It is easy to laugh at the seriousness of the ideal; easier still to put one's finger on omissions. Mr. Saintsbury voices one criticism when he observes that Arnold should have added the words "thoughts" and "feelings" to "subject" and "action." To accept Arnold's canon literally is to leave out whole libraries of poetry. What, for example, becomes of lyric poetry? On the other hand, if we study the spirit of the prefaces,

it becomes clear that Arnold includes by implication
"thoughts" and "feelings" as integral elements of
the "actions." No one can believe, for example,
that Arnold meant to focus upon the slaying of Dun-
can without emphasis upon the thoughts and feelings
incident to Macbeth's passion. This is impossible.
The words "emotion" and "affection" occur too
often in the *Prefaces* to permit this notion.

If indeed by "thoughts" and "feelings" we refer
to the province of lyric and subjective poetry, it may
be admitted that Arnold makes no study of this.
Obviously, throughout the *Prefaces* he is not speaking of lyric poetry. Moreover, in the *Preface of
1854* he declares definitely that the relation of his
theories to lyric poetry is another story. Unluckily,
it is a story which he never relates. His conceptions
of laws for more subjective poetry must be gathered
together from other sources: from letters, and chance
comments. The results are sketchy, but suggestive.
In all his analyses of poetry Arnold was inclined to
underestimate "feelings," but not to the extent nor
in precisely the way which the critics of the *Prefaces*
have assumed.

As conscious illustrations of his theories of subject
and action Arnold wrote two poems: *Sohrab and
Rustum* (1853) and *Balder Dead* (1855). One is
tempted, before examining these, to glance at the
other narrative poems written before the *Prefaces*
appeared. Of the poems of 1849 *Mycerinus* and
The Sick King in Bokhara are too purely reflective
to satisfy the ideals set forth in the *Prefaces*. In

general, however, they have the dignity of theme
and manner which is an inherent part of the theory.
We feel then that, some time before he formulated
his ideas on subject and action, Arnold's natural tendency was towards subjects which possessed an essential greatness or "truth of substance." Even *Tristram and Iseult* (1852), which was published a year
before the first *Preface,* eccentric as it is, suggests
that here is a lofty subject treated with high seriousness. Arnold has certainly not achieved in this poem
"totality of impression." The type of subtle meta-
phor, used later in the conclusions of *Sohrab and
Rustum* and *The Scholar-Gipsy,* is in this poem practically an entire episode: the story of Merlin told
by Iseult to her children. Perhaps Arnold's statement that his version of the legend was superior to
Wagner's and not inferior to Swinburne's is not defensible. On the other hand, *Tristram and Iseult*
is not, as Mr. Stedman says, "an obscure, monot-
onous variation upon a well-worn theme." It is
something more than that. And for us, its interest
lies in the high seriousness which seems to fore-
shadow the more conscious manner of the later
poems, those written in definite illustration of the
Prefaces.

These, *Sohrab and Rustum* and *Balder Dead,* we
can test fairly by Arnold's own canons. Of these
one may ask the questions raised by Arnold in the
Prefaces: Are these actions which appeal to the
great, primary, human affections? Was the writer
so penetrated with his subjects that everything else

followed, especially high excellence of style and "totality of impression"? Has the author, in each of
these poems, avoided the fault of "separate thoughts
and images"? Has he attained, like the ancients, as
part of the totality of impression, "their noble simplicity and their calm pathos"?

A strict catechism! No one, least of all Arnold
himself, would expect in answer a chorus of assent.

> "I am far indeed," he says, "from making any claim,
> for myself, that I possess this discipline; or for the fol-
> lowing Poems, that they breathe its spirit."

Yet he was hopeful of approval. He felt that he
had made some approach towards his ideals.

> "I think [it]," he wrote his mother of *Sohrab and
> Rustum* in May, 1853, "by far the best thing I have
> yet done, and that it will be generally liked."

He found satisfaction, too, in *Balder Dead*.

> *"Balder,"* he wrote Mrs. Forster, "will consolidate
> the peculiar sort of reputation that I got by *Sohrab and
> Rustum.*"

The subject of *Sohrab and Rustum,* theoretically
at least, engages the primary human affections. Both
Rustum, the father, and Sohrab, the son, are nobly
drawn. The climax of the action, the recognition
scene between father and son, is moving. Some
readers find this episode as effective as certain great
scenes in Shakespeare. Yet no mature student is

likely to compare favourably the theme of *Sohrab and Rustum* with those which, consciously or unconsciously, were Arnold's models. I need hardly remark that neither in conduct nor in tragic situation can this poem be mentioned in the same breath with *Œdipus Rex, King Lear,* or *Macbeth.* Can it even be compared to certain powerful parts of *Childe Harold,* to which Arnold refers so lightly, and which he places outside his category, since it heretically neglects action as its chief concern?

Sohrab and Rustum is, of course, far inferior to the masterpieces of "subject and action." No proof of this is required. The real question is whether the poem, lower in quality as it is, still exemplifies to some extent Arnold's theories. Well, it is clear that Arnold was, in one sense, penetrated with his subject. No one, as the *Letters* show, could have felt more deeply the relation of father and son; and the particular expression of it which Arnold celebrates here, and which he drew out from the obscurity of Malcolm's *History of Persia,* had unquestionably stirred his imagination. There is a real tenderness in Arnold's portrayal of the relations between Rustum and Sohrab. Yet, after this is said, there is something in the poem which does not ring true, a fault somewhere. If we analyse this, we shall find that we never forget from one end of the poem to the other that its author is writing with extreme care.

Then we think of the *Prefaces* and realize that what we are conscious of is that Arnold is writing a poem to illustrate a thesis. Now it is one thing, certainly, to be penetrated with a subject unconsciously, and to write as an involuntary result of that penetration, and it is quite another to be penetrated with a subject in order to demonstrate a principle. It may be said, I think, that Shakespeare was penetrated with the subject of *Macbeth* unconsciously; that is, he had no thesis to illustrate. But Arnold, although he is honestly stirred by the story of this father and son, is, after all, writing to make clear the *Preface of 1853*. So the weakness of *Sohrab and Rustum* is that of conscious art, and conscious art must ever give forth, even if ever so slightly, an impression of insincerity. Arnold's theories limit his performance.

In addition to this general weakness, some of the more special tenets of the theory are not fully realized. It will be recalled that one law of the theory of subject and action was that excellence of style should follow as a matter of course from the greatness of the subject. But it does not,—at least not in *Sohrab and Rustum*. Sometimes, indeed, the reader wonders whether in this poem style does not rather control the subject. For the most effective poetry in *Sohrab and Rustum* does not arise naturally out of the great episodes, but seems often to be connected with things outside the action of the poem. How, for example, do the beautiful passages on the Oxus rise inevitably from the action? Or how, on the other side, may it be said that the recognition scene brings with it the best poetry of the piece? The fact is that the power of the poem is due less to emotional scenes, great actions, expressing themselves in a style of high excellence, than to certain splendid passages not too closely connected with the action. We are constantly impressed in reading *Sohrab and Rustum,* not by the working of any such law, but far more than this by Arnold's marvellous elaboration of figures of speech, and by his sustained nobility of manner. He himself has related how he achieved these qualities by careful workmanship.

Certainly it is for these virtues that we re-read *Sohrab and Rustum,* and not for the sake of greatness of action conjoined with greatness of style. We remember the descriptions of nature; we forget what Sohrab said. We remember the Oxus; we forget the fight. We remember the similes of the pearl-diver, the eagle, and the Pekinese workman; we forget who Zal and Peran-Wisa were; what they thought and what they did. It is ironical, perhaps, that, after Arnold's pains, what takes us back to this poem is something very like "separate thoughts and images." The story dims in our minds, but not so passages like the following:

> Then with weak hasty fingers, Sohrab loosed
> His belt, and near the shoulder bared his arm,
> And show'd a sign in faint vermilion points
> Prick'd; as a cunning workman, in Pekin,
> Pricks with vermilion some clear porcelain vase,
> An emperor's gift—at early morn he paints,
> And all day long, and, when night comes, the lamp
> Lights up his studious forehead and thin hands—
> So delicately prick'd the sign appear'd.

Theory and Practice

In the same way, we lack conviction that the whole passage descriptive of Sohrab's death rises naturally into a high excellence of style, but we do remember three beautiful lines, perfect in themselves:

> Unwillingly the spirit fled away
> Regretting the warm mansion which it left,
> And youth, and bloom, and this delightful world.

The similes in *Sohrab and Rustum* will remain for many readers the most delightful parts of the poem. But they have not the inevitableness of those similes which must have been in Arnold's mind. If we compare them with those of the *Iliad*, say that of the fly, or the simile of the stars, we feel still more the deliberateness of Arnold's manner. He has told us how certain similes he tried to orientalize, in order to make them seem more integral. This conscious effort, in spite of skilful handling, is evident. More and more we regard the similes not as inherent in the texture of the poem but as cleverly inserted.

Arnold is guilty, then, of the weakness he condemns: separate thoughts and images. Yes, in a measure, but they are very different, after all, from the types of separate thoughts and images which he dislikes so heartily. What he censured were the utterly detached images of such a poet as Keats. One may select stanzas from Keats's narrative or semi-narrative poems which might be regarded as in themselves separate lyrics. Thus these lines would be placed in their proper context, unless one knows his Keats well, with difficulty:

O Melancholy, linger here awhile!
O Music, Music, breathe despondingly!
O Echo, Echo, from some sombre isle,
Unknown, Lethaean, sigh to us—O sigh!
Spirits in grief, lift up your heads, and smile.

And so on. The lines are taken almost at random from the narrative poem, *Isabella*. Keats loses himself in an ecstasy of melody. Often the final impression of one of his poems is that of a protracted lyric, its various parts linked by a thread of narrative. Arnold's "separate thoughts and images" are not of this variety. They are, of course, less felicitous, and belong to a colder world of poetry. But they are different, too, in that they are not discursive and unrestrained. If they are not as inevitable as Homer's, they are at least far more so than Keats's, and, indeed, more so than those of most nineteenth-century poets. A final conclusion must be, then, that although Arnold has not attained the perfect interweaving of action and imagery of his models, he has, nevertheless, avoided that complete detachment of imagery from action which he disliked in modern poetry.

This is to admit that he has secured in some degree his desired "totality of impression." The final effect is injured by his consciousness of manner, and his inability to make his language of high excellence rise naturally out of the great action, but, when all is said, *Sohrab and Rustum* conveys a certain singleness of impression. The river Oxus, the nobility of the characters, the inexorable Fate, the sustained loftiness of tone, and the river Oxus, once more, at the end,—at once the symbol of half-hinted destinies and the curtain of the poem—all these create a total impression of grandeur,—yes, of "noble simplicity and calm pathos."

Balder Dead is not notably different as an illustration of Arnold's theories. What has been said of *Sohrab and Rustum* is in general true of the later poem; taken together these two represent a particular stage in Arnold's poetic development. Possibly the "great actions" of Hoder and Hermoder seem even less vital than those of the old Persian tale. There is a remoteness about the whole poem, although this is also its charm. *Balder Dead* does on the whole engage the primary human affections less than *Sohrab and Rustum*. On the other hand, it is less mannered; the similes are less intrusive; and its "totality of impression" is more assured than that of *Sohrab and Rustum*.

We have traced the application of Arnold's poetic theories in the poems which appeared before the *Preface of 1853* and the *Preface of 1854,* supposing that in 1849 these notions had taken root in his mind. And more definitely we have examined the two poems which he himself declared were written in support of his theories. It remains then, in connection with this first theory of "subject and action," to notice briefly another application of this conception of poetry. This was an extraordinary attempt to incorporate these laws of subject and action in a play which was Greek in subject, Greek in manner, Greek in form, and English only in language. The ill-fated *Merope* appeared in 1858, and with it another *Preface* which stressed still more the importance of the "subject." *Merope's* failure was almost spectacular. It has been justly called a wax flower. If this play is a normal product of Arnold's theories, let us have none of them! *Merope* proves nothing except the futility of writing a Greek play in English for modern readers. But we must not take *Merope* too seriously as an illustration of the theory of "subject and action." It was a *tour 'de force,* and Arnold was inclined to speak of it playfully:

> "I have no intention," he wrote his mother, "of producing, like Euripides, seventy dramas in this style, but shall now turn to something wholly different."

The only poems by which to test fairly Arnold's use of his own theories of "subject and action" are *Sohrab and Rustum* and *Balder Dead.*

During the latter part of his life Arnold continued to amplify the principles of subject and action. References to the theory occur in all three of the series of *Essays in Criticism.* But during these later years the emphasis shifted decisively to another principle which we are to study, the principle that poetry is a "criticism of life." This phrase, which came to mean so much, Arnold employed in literary criticism. It was, in addition, a guide for him in the creation of his own poetry.

The idea in its perfected forms Arnold states in the first two series of *Essays in Criticism.* Here may be found, with characteristic repetitions and many examples from European literatures, the chief definitions of poetry as "a criticism of life," together with analyses of other aspects of the conception: "natural magic"; "high seriousness"; and "moral interpretation." It is interesting to trace its development from more rudimentary reflections on poetry. Arnold had pondered much before he finally spoke the phrase "criticism of life." He seems to have thought first of poetry as an interpreter. "The grand power of poetry," he says in the essay on *Maurice de Guérin,* "is its interpretative power." Then he began to distinguish between two kinds of interpretation, that which explains the natural world, and that which explains the moral world.

"Poetry," he declares, "interprets in two ways; it interprets by expressing, with magical felicity the physiognomy and movement of the outward world, and it interprets by expressing, with inspired conviction, the ideas and laws of man's moral and spiritual nature. In other words," he concludes, "poetry is interpretative both by having *natural magic* in it, and by having *moral profundity.*"

This cleavage has been thought metaphysical. Modern science and psychology have destroyed such distinctions. Arnold was under the influence of the out-worn theories concerning the nature of the mind. But, if artificial, or even false, the separation of poets who are interested in the outward world and those who are interested in the inward world is a convenient one. The italicized words came to be catchwords in the theory. Arnold kept dividing poets, in his literary criticism, according to this distinction. Keats, he feels, has "natural magic" to excess; Shelley has it hardly at all. Wordsworth is great primarily because of his "moral profundity." Shakespeare's power resides in his mastery of both "natural magic" and also "moral profundity."

So the phrase which was to distract so many critics was almost spoken. Arnold had not yet invented it, but it was soon to appear. Obviously, one may reasonably bind these two worlds of "natural magic" and "moral profundity" together. So linked, they represent the contribution of all poets, and they may be said to be two complementary aspects of life itself. What the great poets do then, in varying degrees, and with varying emphasis on one or the other aspect, is to reflect life—the life of nature and the life of man's spirit. So that poetry interprets "life." Soon the phrase is spoken, in the essay on *Joubert,* during a discussion of men of genius as opposed to men of talent.

> "Let us be sure," Arnold says, "what we mean, in literature, by *famous.* There are the famous men of genius in literature,—the Homers, Dantes, Shakespeares: of them we need not speak; their praise is for ever and ever. Then there are the famous men of ability in literature: their praise is in their own generation. And what makes this difference? The work of the two orders of men is at bottom the same—*a criticism of life.* The end and aim of all literature, if one considers it attentively, is, in truth, nothing but that."

As every student of Matthew Arnold knows,

around these four words as a definition of poetry, has raged a storm of ridicule. The objections are in sum only two. One is that such a definition fails to distinguish between poetry and prose. The other objection, to be considered presently, is that such a canon has no practical value. In reply to the first objection it must be admitted that if Arnold had stopped with the phrase itself, the objection would have been justified. As the four words stand, they are vague. (Prose, he admits, reflects outward and inward worlds.) As a matter of fact, Arnold went much farther. He recognized that a distinction must be drawn between the criticism of life found in prose and that in verse. He made this distinction by amplifying and explaining the phrase. Here is a complete definition, printed in *The Study of Poetry* in 1880: Poetry is "a criticism of life" under *"the conditions fixed for such a criticism by the laws of poetic truth and poetic beauty."* This conception Arnold states more positively in speaking of Burns:

> "For supreme poetical success," he says, "more is required than the powerful application of ideas to life; it must be an application under the conditions fixed by the laws of poetic truth and poetic beauty."

But what are these laws? Is Arnold hiding behind a generalization? If one insists on a detailed explanation of the entire theory in any particular passage in Arnold's writings, he will be disappointed. This is not Arnold's way. One must bind his theories together. As I read I have tried to guess what

145

Arnold's conception of these laws was. I am inclined to think that he means the old qualities already
mentioned: "high seriousness" and "truth of substance." Perhaps he has in mind also the more conventional attributes of poetry: style, manner, accent,
diction, movement. This is true; both such guesses
are accurate. In the essay on Byron occurs Arnold's
own statement of these laws:

> "Truth and seriousness of substance and matter,
> felicity and perfection of diction and manner, as these
> are exhibited in the best poets, are what constitute a
> criticism of life made in conformity with the laws of
> poetic truth and poetic beauty."

If the definition of poetry as "a criticism of life"
is examined in the light of these amplifications, one
has less patience with those who object that the
theory does not distinguish between poetry and prose.
The component parts of the theory are scattered, but
they make up, I think, a definite conception concerning poetry. Poetry in this theory is distinguished
from prose. Thus to reply to Arnold that everything written, including Mother Goose, is "a criticism
of life" is idle; to say that poetry is an imaginative
not a critical process, and cannot, therefore, be "criticism," is to mistake Arnold's meaning. The crux
of the matter is that readers have been inclined to
study the phrase "criticism of life" *per se*. It is, after
all, like "culture" and "sweetness and light," a catch-
phrase. One must probe beneath the words to grasp
Arnold's whole meaning.

The other objection to Arnold's theory of poetry as "a criticism of life" is concerned with the negation of its practical value. The use of a theory of poetry is in the main two-fold. It may help us to judge poetry; and it may help us to write poetry. The famous definitions of poetry by Milton, by Coleridge, by Wordsworth, the critics say, have aided men in both these respects. In reading or in writing poetry we instinctively test by their definitions. This, critics maintain, the vagueness of the "criticism of life" theory forbids. It is, of course, difficult to say how much readers are guided in their judgments of literature by this theory of Arnold's. Personally I fancy that in reading poetry there are as many people who think of poetry as "a criticism of life" as there are those who remind themselves constantly that poetry is "simple, sensuous, and passionate." One cannot go far in this direction. But everyone knows that for Arnold himself the theory constituted a very reliable touchstone for recording verdicts on books. He recurs to it constantly in all the *Essays in Criticism*. Its various phases of "high seriousness" and "truth of substance"; the emphasis on style, and on ideas,—these tests have brought from Arnold some memorable criticisms of literature.

Arnold has applied directly or indirectly the "criticism of life" theory to about two dozen poets. In every case he has arrived at estimates which, if they do not convince, challenge us, if we can, to do better. Who will deny the value of Arnold's analyses by this method of Chaucer? Burns? Keats?

Chaucer, he says "is not one of the great classics," for he lacks the high and excellent seriousness of Dante. Villon is great, but *fitfully* so. Dryden and Pope are the classics of our *prose;* they do not conform to the laws of poetic truth and beauty. So the judgments continue, all moulded by this theory. Arnold uses, of course, his touchstones of poetry, applying as a test to unknown poetry the acknowledged great poetry of the past. Yet the "touchstone" method is at bottom an aspect of the theory that poetry is "a criticism of life." He selects for his touchstones passages which have "natural magic" and "moral profundity."

> "Burns, like Chaucer, comes short of the high seriousness of the great classics, and the virtue of matter and manner which goes with that high seriousness is wanting to his work." "Milton," Arnold goes on to say in the next essay, "from one end of *Paradise Lost* to the other, is in his diction and rhythm constantly a great artist in the great style."

Again, in "natural magic" Keats ranks with Shakespeare. Certainly in literary criticism the theory seems to have some practical value. The defender of Arnold's "criticism of life" theory may, I think, quietly reply to these objectors: "It *is* useful."

As in the case of readers, no one may say how deeply poets have been influenced in writing by Arnold's theory. But here again I fancy that it has constrained writers about as much as most definitions of poetry; namely, very little. The point in this connection is that it aided Arnold. As in the case of the "subject and action" theory, he wrote poetry with this ideal in mind. He never tried to illustrate this theory so definitely as the other in writing *Sohrab and Rustum* and *Balder Dead*. The belief, however, that poetry was "a criticism of life" permeated him as he composed poetry. It is identified with what is most suggestive in him as a thinker. "To know the best that is known and thought in the world" is but another aspect of the "criticism of life" theory. The noblest poetry is that which reflects the noblest ideas of life. "For poetry," he says, "the idea is everything. . . . Poetry attaches its emotion to the idea." Poetry is concerned with ideas which teach us how to live.

It is fair, then, as in the case of "subject and action" to test his theory in practice. Has Arnold's poetry "natural magic"? "Moral profundity"? Has it "truth and seriousness of substance and matter, felicity and perfection of diction and manner"? Is it, in fine, "a criticism of life"? "Truth and seriousness of substance and matter" are allied closely to "moral profundity." Something will be said later of Arnold's "diction and manner." So that the tests with which we are mainly concerned now are those of "natural magic" and "moral profundity." Does he possess these? And, if so, in what measure?

It is evident that the poetry of Arnold has little claim to "natural magic." Arnold is incapable, like Keats, who is his example of this quality, of abandoning himself to the joy of nature for its own sake. He has little of the ecstatic rejoicing in nature which he describes in the essay *On the Study of Celtic Literature.* Nor does he even yield to more restrained raptures, like his beloved De Guérin. Instead of this feeling, he experiences a calm pleasure in nature. His communion with her is sincere and tender. He turns to her for refuge. His poetry is filled with haunting sounds and sights from nature. In *Sohrab and Rustum* there are the river and the ocean; in *A Summer Night* the star-lit sky; and in *The Strayed Reveller* "the cool night-wind . . . glimmering water . . . dreaming woods." It is Swinburne who speaks of the perfection of Arnold's landscape:

> Soon will the musk carnations break and swell,
> Soon shall we have gold-dusted snapdragon,
> Sweet-William with his homely cottage smell,
> And stocks in fragrant blow;
> Roses that down the alleys shine afar,
> And open, jasmine-muffled lattices,
> And groups under the dreaming garden-trees,
> And the full moon, and the white evening star.

This is not "natural magic," as Arnold conceives of it, but it is joy of a kind, a tranquil joy in nature as a source of strength. Arnold speaks of "the power with which Wordsworth feels the joy offered to us in nature." The saying is true of himself. He makes us feel the joy which nature will give for the asking. But this implies that Arnold's attitude towards nature is Wordsworthian. It is; Arnold is a Wordsworthian. No other modern except, possibly,

Goethe, affected him so deeply. Arnold rarely if ever shows us a gleam of "natural magic," but in her, like Wordsworth, he feels the joy of "a presence."

What of "moral profundity"? It is a heavy term, far less happy than other phrases of Arnold's. What Arnold means, however, is clear. As he has been speaking of the world of nature, he is now speaking of the world of man's spirit. Through "moral profundity" he conceives of the ideas on life which man's spirit and mind have evolved, especially of the ideas which deal with man's problems and destiny; which connect him with the unseen; and which console and strengthen him. The idea is the thing, the idea touched with emotion. There are, naturally, varying degrees of "moral profundity," but in so far as concern with ideas is a mark of this quality, Arnold has attained it. Hardly a poem of his is free from ideas, that is, from reflections on life. His ideal seems to be, like the title of one of his lyrics, *Austerity of Poetry:*

> Such, poets, is your bride, the Muse! young, gay,
> Radiant, adorn'd outside; a hidden ground
> Of thought and of austerity within.

Other titles—*Morality, Self-Dependence, The Buried Life*—keep reminding us that we are in the realms of thought. Mr. Ward has commented upon Arnold's fondness for making poetry out of intellectual types. Empedocles, Obermann, the Scholar-Gipsy, and the rest, all suffer from the malady of thought. Themes which have moved other poets to forgetfulness or rapture, stir in Arnold ideas. The anguish of Mycerinus deadens into self-possession; the passion of Iseult dwindles into a disquisition on modern unrest; and the poem *Immortality* ends with lines identical with a passage on immortality in Arnold's prose. So in the *Switzerland* lyrics it is the idea of separation which disturbs him, and not the actual pain of parting. Barring a few verses on the deaths of his pets, Arnold wrote no poems on the unusual, the esoteric, or the trivial. Never do we encounter fancy or caprice; and all too seldom is there lightness of touch. Indeed, most feelings in Arnold's poetry may be called intellectual: calm from the influence of nature, melancholy before the enigma of life.

He has, then, in so far as was consistent with his gifts, "moral profundity." He has not, however, by temperament, the power of "natural magic." He succeeds in interpreting the inward world, but not, judged by the highest poetry, in revealing the outer world. Is then his poetry, by his own standards, "a criticism of life"? I think that Arnold, with due modesty, would have considered it such. For, although he admires the "natural magic" in Shakespeare, Keats, and other poets, and although he regards it as essential to poetry of the very first grade, it is also clear that he thinks of poetry as being often admirable without it. The *idea* is the thing! Here once more we feel his kinship with Wordsworth. In the remarkable passage in *Maurice de Guérin* he hints that "moral profundity" will often overshadow "natural magic."

> "Poetry," he says, "is interpretative both by having *natural magic* in it, and by having *moral profundity*. In both ways it illuminates man; it gives him a satisfying sense of reality; it reconciles him with himself and the universe. . . . But it is observable that in the poets who unite both kinds, the latter (the moral) usually ends by making itself the master."

As an example of this tendency Arnold cites Wordsworth. In Arnold, too, the "moral" predominates. Arnold's poetry is not then in a complete sense "a criticism of life," but it does reasonably fulfil one part of the theory.

Such are the great principles in Arnold's poetic theory: "subject and action" and poetry as "a criticism of life"; and such are the results of applying them to his own poetry. The last part of this essay should at least remark minor canons for poetry which Arnold held. These are difficult to assemble, and some of them are inextricably joined to the principles we have studied. Nevertheless, even a brief survey of Arnold's poetic principles would be incomplete without some comment upon them. These are, chiefly, his attitude towards Greek literature; simplicity; restraint; and the technique of metres.

In Arnold's attitude towards Greek literature one discovers another definite attempt to make, in his own poetry, practice conform to theory. Obviously many of the elements in the two great principles had their origin in Greek literature, and Arnold's trial of a Greek play in English has already been mentioned. Arnold took from the Greek subjects, metres, and even a particular manner, and at the same time that he held up the Greek poets as exemplars he wrote poems, besides *Merope,* embodying these characteristics. Arnold's intimacy with Greek literature need not be reiterated here. A reference list which I have kept in reading his prose is made up, for the most part, of his allusions to the classics. One of the most striking is the passage at the beginning of *The Modern Element in Literature.*

> "Even admitting," he says, "to their fullest extent the legitimate demands of our age, the literature of ancient Greece is, even for modern times, a mighty agent of intellectual deliverance; even for modern times, therefore, an object of indestructible interest."

In the essay, *Pagan and Mediæval Religious Sentiment,* may be found the beautiful translation of the fifteenth idyl of Theocritus, and Arnold's commentary upon the age in which it was written. The first series of *Essays in Criticism* concludes with the picture of *Marcus Aurelius,* so eloquent, and so descriptive, if not of Arnold himself, at least of an ideal of his. Other examples are manifold. He writes in 1851 that he is retiring more and more from the modern world and from modern literature. In very different forms of expression Arnold makes clear his absorption in Greek literature. There are the *Notebooks;* the lectures *On Translating Homer;*

154

the sonnet *To a Friend*. The strength of this preference is suggested by a chance remark of Arnold's to
Mr. Thomas Ward: "There is more in one little
volume of André Chénier than in the whole forty
volumes of Hugo."

To test the effect of this ideal in Arnold's own
poetry one should turn to *Merope*, to the *Fragment
of an "Antigone,"* to the *Fragment of Chorus of a
"Dejaneira,"* to *The Strayed Reveller*, and to various
other short poems. Are they Greek in spirit or form?
Swinburne says that no poet has ever come so near
the perfect Greek as Arnold, but this statement
occurs in the famous eulogy on Arnold in the *Fortnightly*. Matthew Arnold's debt to Greek literature
is worthy of an essay in itself. It is enough to observe here that the great enemy to Arnold's fulfilment of a Greek ideal in English poetry is, unhappily,
the modern strain in him. He often catches the mood
and the metre of Greek poetry, but his lyric poetry
is intensely subjective and is filled with introspection
concerning modern problems. His poetry is reminiscent of Greek poetry rather than completely under
its spell.

Arnold's emphasis upon simplicity and measure
and restraint was an ideal instinctive in his nature,
strengthened by his reverence for the Greeks and
for Wordsworth. Simplicity is a quality which he
never tires of praising.

> "It is," he says, writing of Celtic literature, "the sim-
> ple passages in poets like Pindar or Dante which are
> perfect, their simplicity being a *poetical* simplicity."

He reveres the simplicity of *Obermann;* he denounces the lack of it in Keats, and in Macaulay. He commends Milton for achieving it, and he likes Scherer, the critic of Milton, for himself praising it in Milton. When we turn to Arnold's poetry we feel that he has made good his own gospel. A noble simplicity is part of the charm of his poetry. He is never guilty of excess. He attains simplicity in various ways, for one, by sustaining through long passages straightforward constructions:

> Sophocles long ago
> Heard it on the Ægean, and it brought
> Into his mind the turbid ebb and flow
> Of human misery; we
> Find also in the sound a thought,
> Hearing it by the distant, northern sea.

Or, he uses monosyllables, one after another:

> If these are yours, if this is what you are,
> Then am I yours, and what you feel, I share.

Arnold's simplicity of language is not always edifying. At its worst it is blunt and stiff:

> Who prop, thou ask'st, in these bad days, my mind?

Or, sometimes, this poetical simplicity is merely bad prose:

> Time, so complain'd of
> Who to no one man
> Shows partiality
> Brings round to all men
> Some undimm'd hours.

But Arnold's simplicity at its best may give us lines like these:

> Sweep in the sounding stillness of the night.

Or:

> The unplumb'd, salt, estranging sea.

Coupled with Arnold's love of simplicity is his emphasis upon measure or restraint. This, too, was derived from the ancients, but, in addition, was inherent in his nature. Arnold's attitude of reflection, of balance, of moderation, was less an attitude towards poetry than an attitude towards life. "The nice sense of measure," Arnold says, "is certainly not one of Nature's gifts to her children." To measure, then, Arnold will hold fast. This habit of poise, of calm method, was an essential virtue in his life. This is not, however, always an unmixed blessing in his poetry. If Arnold would, I often think, more often forget himself! The restraint of his poetry is not so much in one poem as everywhere. One feels that Arnold in writing poetry is the victim of his own critical mind. He watches his own work too closely, and becomes self-conscious. Whenever he writes, he is the talented, but self-restrained English gentleman. Wordsworth's genius transcended his poetical theory, but Arnold's talent could not perform a similar service for the poems written as "a criticism of life."

The last detail in Arnold's poetic theory, his attitude towards metrical technique, has been often held against him. Many critics have denied him melody of verse, and indeed his success as a poet is certainly not due to a mastery of metrical forms. He nowhere speaks against the importance of metre. He says little of it, in one way or the other. He discusses briefly in *Maurice de Guérin,* in *The French Play in London,* and in the *Irish Essays* fundamental verse forms. He decries the Alexandrine and the heroic couplet, and declares that blank verse is the proper vehicle for the best poetry. The *Letters* give little hint of a deep interest in metres. In fact, his silence on metres makes some readers think, perhaps unfairly, that his underlying principle for style in lyric poetry is not study of verse forms but reliance on his old faith: that excellence of style follows inevitably excellence of subject.

Certainly his silence on technique has counted against him. A reasonable conclusion after reading some of Arnold's poetry is that he has a defective ear. Arnold is the author of some dreadful lines. Mr. Oliver Elton reproaches him, and rightly, for the line:

> My melancholy, sciolists say—

Other examples abound. There is the beginning of the sonnet on *Rachel* and the extraordinary sestet of *The Good Shepherd With the Kid.* And in *The Future* Arnold writes of man:

> Only the tract where he sails
> He wots of.

Perhaps such minute strictures are unfair. But in *The New Sirens* "dawning" strives without appreciable success to rhyme with "morning," and, as Mr.

Saintsbury has pointed out, there is the omnipresent monosyllable, "Ah!" Yet, without subtleties, Arnold is workmanlike, as in *The Scholar-Gipsy* and *Thyrsis;* and in slow movements of the sombre iambic he is often very effective. His irregular, unrhymed stanzas are both good and bad within the same poem, as in *Rugby Chapel,* where the verse is anapestic.

In fact, in spite of the bad lines, I wonder whether Arnold did not have theories about metre and rhythm which he did not pronounce publicly. He was certainly able to produce, when he wished, verse with subtle melodies and rhythms. *The Forsaken Merman, The Scholar-Gipsy,* and *Thyrsis* do not support the theory that he had a bad ear. Then there are the numerous adventures in verse: say, *The Strayed Reveller, Philomela,* or *Rugby Chapel.* A study of these leads me to suggest a heretical theory that Arnold even tried some of the tricks which have such vogue today. Certainly he was fond, for their own sake, of unrhymed lines, of assonance, of irregular rhythms. Modern writers of verse are frequently finding that orthodox Victorians tried their hands at what have been thought to be ultra-modern metrical experiments. "Undiscovered imagists" is a phrase we hear often, as students of metres look back at earlier poets more carefully. One fact, at least, I know: a few modern poets turn to Arnold's metres for suggestion and guidance. This certainly means something. Perhaps Arnold had not thought the subject through, and was reticent about stating his theories in print. And perhaps this tendency explains some of the bad lines. He was not always successful in his experiments. In any case certain passages in Arnold's poetry resemble the free verse of today. I think it perilous to avow that Arnold was indifferent to metre, or that he had a limited conception of its possibilities.*

Finally, then, in trying to illustrate his poetic principles in practice Arnold had reasonable success. He kept the faith that was in him. I think it untrue, as Mr. Stedman says, that in his lyric poetry he refuted his own theories, or, as Mr. Gates believes, that his theories gave way before his innate romanticism. Both these criticisms are based on the assumption that the *Prefaces,* and similar statements, referred to lyric poetry. It is hard to put together all of Arnold's theories, but it should be done before passing judgment. His fault through it all was that he was self-conscious. He could not forget, apparently, that he was illustrating a theory. But he attempted a difficult feat, and he achieved much.

---

* I am indebted to Miss Amy Lowell, who is a constant student of both the essays and the poetry, for an interesting statement concerning this point. It will be recalled that one of Miss Lowell's first sonnets begins, in reference to Arnold:

> Dear Master, it is years since first my mind
> Came under sway of thine. . . .

Miss Lowell notes that "Matthew Arnold did write free verse, or cadenced verse, which is the much better title for the form, but what he attempted was the effect of Greek verse, as he says in his preface to *Empedocles on Etna.* . . . His best known poem in cadenced verse is *Philomela.* . . . He happens, like Henley, to be one of the unacknowledged precursors of the modern free verse movement, but, as I see it to-day, the direct inspiration for the form came from the *French Symbolistes.*"

Victorian Poetry of Social Unrest

Victorian Poetry of Social Unrest

It is difficult to go far in Victorian prose without encountering the anguish of the poor. Even if the reader takes refuge in the novels of the indifferent or in the poetry of the light-hearted, yet, just as when Tristram hid, there is the blood for witness. Although he reads only Hellenic Morris or mediæval Rossetti, the shadow of human misery darkens the page: there is *The Voice of Toil,* and there is *Jenny.* Always creeps in "the eternal note of sadness." As the reader lives again in the age of the industrial revolution, he finds himself in the attitude of Carlyle, "sitting among a thousand dead dogs": the sins against the poor weigh him down; their forgotten griefs stain his imagination. If he turns to Carlyle, he finds *Past and Present* with its tales of women who have sodden their own children. If he reads Kingsley, he cannot escape *Yeast* and *Alton Locke,* two microcosms of suffering; there is little to choose, indeed, between the village revel and the city gin-shop. Later William Morris tells indirectly the same tale: the idle singer of an empty day flees to an impossible paradise, forgetting in his palace of art, if he can, the hell about him.

> The end is everywhere,
> Art still has truth, take refuge there!

Even the smiling Matthew Arnold observes ironically that the murderess "Wragg is in custody." Victorian prose-writers are by turns cynical or merry, but they never still the voices of those that mourn and will not be comforted.

Much of the Victorian prose concerned with social questions is frankly practical. It describes abuses, and proposes reforms to be legislated. Kingsley demands sanitary betterment for the agricultural poor; Hughes recommends a new community on the Susquehanna; even Carlyle, in spite of his doubts in the efficacy of mere legislation, feels that new laws should be enacted. Some of these pamphlets, like Carlyle's or Kingsley's, still burn with their old ardour. *Latter-Day Pamphlets* or certain of Kingsley's prefaces may still arouse emotion. But much of the writing on these subjects seems burnt out. We know that the reforms which were urged so fiercely are accomplished, and we are amused at the motheaten political economy which permeates these pages. What the friends of mankind were asking in 1850 is by no means the burden of their petition in 1923. The issues have shifted ground. The problems appear archaic, and our interest in them is somewhat like that of the antiquarian.

But this is not true of the poetry which reflects Victorian social unrest. By its nature it is less polemical, and freer from ideas of political reform. And, most of all, the poetry gives poignant expression to the *feelings* of those under the oppression of the social wrongs. If we are not much concerned with obsolete political economy, we are, nevertheless, even more capable now of comprehending the griefs of those who toil and mourn and die. This, at least,

164

the war has done for us. "I met a hundred men on
the road to Delhi"—or Flanders, or the Argonne—
"and they were all my brothers." Brotherhood is
being proved daily, and some are likely to have it,
if not willingly, on compulsion. Carlyle's sardonic
anecdote of the woman who demonstrated her sister-
hood by bestowing typhus fever upon fine ladies has
some point today. Modern thought is breaking
down the barriers between classes, the barriers that
these poor workers of the past felt so keenly. And
their feelings about the injustice of the social order
move us, apart from certain rhapsodical passages in
Carlyle and Kingsley, most deeply through their
poetry. Although each has the same theme, Hood's
Song of the Shirt has outlived Kingsley's *Cheap
Clothes and Nasty,* and the reason is not in the
former's euphemism of title. Hood's lyric is tense
with feeling; it is a cry of despair, piercing, bitter.
Call it, if you will, an ugly poem. It was, at any
rate, wrung from the soul of one who understood
sweat of the body, sweat of the brain—and despair.
For the basic ideas, for reforms, for the legislation
connected with Victorian social unrest, it is well to
examine the prose. But to be attuned to the emotions of the period we must know its poetry of social
unrest.

Every critic of the Victorian poets likes to point
out their pessimism. Ruskin's dismay in *Modern
Painters* concerning poets either adrift in faith or
tugging at their anchors was justified. Aside from
Tennyson and Browning and a few others endowed

with a kind of healthy energy, nineteenth-century poetry is apt to reflect the smoky existence seen by George Eliot, who thought that on the whole life was a bad business. In their turn Arnold and Clough, the "younger poets," prolong the minor key. Critics feel this depression, but they have been inclined to over-emphasize its philosophical aspects. Naturally, science and the revaluation of old faiths were at the bottom of this, especially in intellectual men. But there was also a connection between this pessimism and social unrest. Science had made theologians wonder about the next life, but the industrial revolution left no doubt that certain conditions in this one were intolerable. Radicals are too apt to think that Victorian social unrest was represented among the poets solely by Tennyson and Browning. Utterly different from their laments is the poetry of more obscure poets whose bitterness of feeling and expression is startlingly like the mood of the oppressed who write today. Carlyle points out how the ground tone of a passage in a German opera was based upon the cry of the people: "Bread, bread!" And in the midst of all the art and philosophical speculation of the century is heard this cry.

Some nineteenth-century poets even made their Muses servants to political reform. By so doing they courted oblivion, of course, and in the larger sense are forgotten. In the *Oxford Book of English Verse* may be found just two lyrics by Ebenezer Elliott, "the Burns of Sheffield," and one of these survivals has no hint of Sheffield. It is difficult in

these days to catch anyone reading the lyrics of Eliza
Cook, or the poetry of Thomas Cooper. Perhaps
the bitterness of Elliott and Cooper was a boomerang
which returned and wounded them mortally. Certainly their poetic descriptions of factories did not
help them to put on immortality. Yet these poets
made an impression as a whole which will last. They
were interested in the poor, and depicted the emotions of the poor in verse. The result was not to
create a definite body of poetry dealing with this
theme. Nor was it to raise up a group of poets to
fame, in the fashion that Crabbe's pictures of the
villages made him famous. These men were not
merely bards of humble life, like Bloomfield. The
effect of their poetry was subtler.

First of all these facts proved that poetry could
be made a weapon for social reform.

> "For good or for evil," Frederic Harrison remarks,
> "our literature is now absorbed in the urgent social
> problem, and is become but an instrument in the vast
> field of Sociology,—the science of Society."

Not only did a few poets devote their poetry altogether to industrial issues, but other poets, more
aloof from the actual struggles of the poor, were
affected by the unrest. Its influence created in the
poetry of the age sometimes fierce eddies, as in the
verse of Elliott and Cooper, but it was rather like
an ever-widening ripple that stirred the whole stream
of Victorian poetry. Early in the 'forties William
J. Fox lectured on the writers who were assisting
practically the cause of the poor. Fox's category

was not exhaustive but it included Tennyson, Wordsworth, and Mrs. Browning, none of whom are primarily identified with social reform. If we include these, we may reasonably add many other names which at first seem apart from such questions, even those of Matthew Arnold and Arthur Hugh Clough. Such poets reveal their interest in many ways, sometimes by a lyric, a ballad, or merely a couplet; sometimes, like Tennyson, they allude to these questions in incident and character.

At first glance Tennyson seems rather courtly about the problem of poor-relief. Nevertheless, his poetry reflects real care for the suffering of England. Relatively few of his poems focus exclusively upon the theme, but the reader feels that the problem is constantly in Tennyson's mind. Its influence runs through the *Idylls of the King* like a black weave through gorgeous tapestries. There are hints of the evil in lyrics like *Lady Clara Vere de Vere* and *The Miller's Daughter,* and it stalks like a ghost through certain parts of *Maud.** In *Locksley Hall Sixty Years After* Tennyson's bitterness is akin to Elliott's and Cooper's:

> There the smouldering fire of fever creeps across the
>   rotted floor,
> And the crowded couch of incest in the warrens of the
>   poor.

* There are stanzas in this poem as bitter as anything in Carlyle or Ruskin:
And the vitriol madness flushes up in the ruffian's head,
Till the filthy by-lane rings to the yell of the trampled wife,
And chalk and alum and plaster are sold to the poor for bread,
And the spirit of murder works in the very means of life.

Even in *In Memoriam* the poet's personal grief suggests more general wrongs. There is, he declares:

> A deeper voice across the storm
> Proclaiming social truth shall spread,
> And *justice*.

Arnold and Clough, of course, dwell upon the annals of the poor more faintly. Arnold seems detached; he is less concerned by the lack of bread than by the complacence of the upper middle class, and by the lack of faith. His cure of "culture" is indeed like parmaceti, but Arnold was not insensible to the inward bruise. He understood his Philistine and his "remnant" too well for that. He was alienated by the blind enthusiasms of muscular Christianity and like phenomena, but he was not indifferent to the distresses of the submerged. *A Summer Night* reveals a sympathy for those who toil that is deep and comprehending. Clough's period of devotion to Carlyle attests his study of the problems of the poor; as do his active philanthropy, and certain portions of his prose. In the last analysis, perhaps, these questions were merely another factor in Clough's introspection about God and life; the issue of poverty makes for him the solution of these great problems still more difficult. But, aside from this philosophical consideration, some poems, notably *Life is Struggle,* are reminiscent of the suffering of the lower classes. And *The Bothie of Tober-na-Vuolich*, although in gay hexameters, debates political issues. Both Arnold and Clough hear, even if far-off, the cry of "Bread."

If the social unrest did not affect a writer's work as a whole, as it did Tennyson's, or indirectly, as it did the poetry of Arnold and Clough, it expressed itself, in some other poets, in one or two poems pulsating with feeling. William Morris would wave a red flag in a Socialist demonstration and write tracts on political economy, but he would not make his poetry as a whole the medium for this phase of his life. Yet it seems as if his *Voice of Toil* possessed a fervour absent from his romantic lyrics. Or we hear this in *The Day Is Coming:*

> For then, laugh not, but listen to this strange tale of
> mine,
> All folk that are in England shall be better lodged than
> swine.

The lack of more poetry from Morris on a theme so dear to him is comprehensible if we recollect his ideals for art, whether in painting or in poetry. An artist like Morris was likely to see more clearly than a politician-poet like Ebenezer Elliott that poetry was not the ideal weapon for combating the Malthusian doctrine. The best statement of Morris's social ideals may be found in his prose. Nevertheless, we have expression in his poetry of sympathy for the wrongs of the poor.

For another reason Charles Kingsley's verse records the unrest but intermittently. The reason is that Kingsley was not inclined to take himself seriously as a poet. In *The Saint's Tragedy* he depicts the twelfth century, and in the pictures of Elizabeth's work among the poor he is unquestionably thinking of modern England. But after this youthful poem, his poetry became engrossed with literary or semi-literary subjects. His anger against oppression found relief in novel or pamphlet. His hurried genius spent itself in prose, pleading, exhorting, after the manner of his teacher, Carlyle. Kingsley was incapable of forgetting the misery of the poor. It appears on almost every page of his novels. He bore an active part in the assault on English indifference. He, more than Maurice, was the leader of the Christian Socialists, and many remember him now chiefly as "Parson Lot," with his violent letters to the newspapers of the day. He was certain that a revolution in England was imminent. But his enthusiasm in this cause was more at home in prose. There is a good deal of the boy in Kingsley; his rages and satisfactions are so irrepressible, and often so out of proportion to their objects: he is equally frantic against the Oxford Movement and against corsets. He is determined to slay his dragons, but to poetry as a means to his end he resorts only occasionally. When he does, we have a *sæva indignatio,* burning fiercely, like a flash of Carlyle's lightning.

Most of these poems seem like outcries of the moment. They are set into the novels at crescent points of Kingsleyan wrath, as if their author felt that prose was too tepid for his purpose; as if he believed that his anger rightly demanded poetry. At the climax of his denunciation of the wrongs of the agricultural poor in *Yeast* appears the ballad of *The*

Bad Squire. And *Alton Locke* ends with the song:

> Weep, weep, weep, and weep
> For pauper, dolt, and slave;
> Hark! from wasted moor and fen,
> Feverous alley, workhouse den,
> Swells the wail of Englishmen!
> "Work! or the grave."

Kingsley was at his best in a kind of local ballad, based on his own experience in Devon, such as *The Three Fishers* or *The Sands of Dee*. If he lives at all as a poet, it will be through a few lyrics of this kind. For Kingsley harboured the illusion that contemplative poetry as a type was doomed to pass. He was conscious of his own inability to write reflective poetry, and his later poems depended for their effects on a certain lilt, and on a rather hearty enthusiasm. He writes poetry like prose with gusto. When his theme became, instead of buccaneers, or outlaws, the cause of the poor, there resulted poetry like that in *The Bad Squire,* robust in feeling, swift-moving, and ennobled by real sympathy. Kingsley's poetry of social unrest is, above all, uncompromisingly sincere.

Another poet, less intimately acquainted than Kingsley with the living conditions of the wretched, contrived to write a few lyrics of the poor, which achieved for him fame in his own time, and also some degree of immortality. This poet was Thomas Hood, "the witty and the tender Hood." Hood did not have Kingsley's passion for righteousness. He was a journalist, not a clergyman. But their poetry on these themes has much in common. In both there is the same anger, and the same fervour. Kingsley was affected by Hood, especially by the fact that Hood's best poetry dealt with the suffering of the poor.

"Is this a time," he asks in *Alton Locke,* "to listen to the voices of singing men and singing women? . . . Which of poor Hood's lyrics have an equal chance of immortality with *The Song of the Shirt* and *The Bridge of Sighs,* rising, as they do, right out of the depths of that Inferno, sublime from their very simplicity? Which of Charles Mackay's lyrics can compare for a moment with the Æschylean grandeur, the terrible rhythmic lilt of his *Cholera Chant?*"

Hood knew something of poverty, but he was not always himself poor. It seems a caprice of fate that this jester, this writer of songs should become dear to the lowest pauper; that a man whose profession was laughter should sing so movingly of tears. But Hood's suit of motley hid sympathy. His grief for the poor was real. In 1815, as merely one instance, he writes to his aunt, very sadly, of the filth and anguish in the slums of London. Even if we read his mirthful doggerel we find frequent allusion to the sorrows of the time. These he tried to fight, for the most part, with jests. But the thought of the lowly is always to be found in his poetry, as when the extravagant fun of *Miss Kilmansegg and Her Precious Leg* throws into sharp relief the death scenes in that poem. Stedman believes that he was

173

able to interpret the popular heart because he himself
was a sufferer. It is extraordinary, when Hood is
re-read from this point of view, how much of his
gaiety seems tremulous. His pity for the wretched
is profound, and his mirth is a cloak. He has the
power of the strong to jest when there is small cause
for rejoicing. His romances also are likely to be
concerned with the unfortunate, his *Dream of
Eugene Aram* being, in effect, a study of the feelings
of a criminal. And, besides the popular lyrics, there
are many poems, such as *The Lady's Dream, The
Workhouse Clock,* and *The Lay of the Labourer,*
which deal solely with the despair of the lower
classes.

The distinction of Hood in this type of poetry
lies in the fact that his verse was actually popular
among the poor. The two lyrics which have survived
he wrote by the merest chance, but they were known
everywhere. He was regarded throughout the length
and breadth of England not merely as a poet who
understood the griefs of the poor, but as one who
had made these griefs singable, and so widely appreciated. An account of the origin of *The Song of the
Shirt* occurs in Jerrold's *Life of Hood:*

> "A wretched woman . . . was charged at the Lam-
> beth police office with having pawned articles belonging
> to her employer. It was shown that she made trousers
> for sevenpence a pair and that the utmost she could
> make was seven shillings a week, which her employers
> looked upon as 'a good living for a woman who had
> herself and two infant children to support.'"

174

Victorian Poetry of Social Unrest

To arouse sympathy one anecdote is worth a book of statistics. The mild interest in this woman Hood changed into aggressive indignation by a poem as simple as it was poignant. *"The Song of the Shirt,"* says a contemporary, "went through the land like wild-fire." It was reprinted in countless journals; it was translated into foreign tongues; it was woven into cotton handkerchiefs; and it was sung in the streets of London. It is impossible to exaggerate the universality of its appeal. It was read by every Englishman. Had Hood written nothing else, he would have always been linked with the down-trodden, as their champion. On Hood's monument we may read: "He Sang the 'Song of the Shirt.' "

The second lyric, *The Bridge of Sighs,* was less popular than *The Song of the Shirt,* but its literary merit was greater. *The Bridge of Sighs* is a dirge; a lament for a girl who drowned herself in preference to making shirts "at three halfpence apiece." This brief poem Browning thought alone in its generation. Even in these lyrics Hood betrays his weakness as a poet. Mr. Saintsbury to the contrary, he is not free from sentimentality. Moreover, he lacks dignity and reticence. He will not endure always, in spite of popular editions of his verse and in spite of his honourable place in anthologies. Nor has he the distinction, like some poets of social unrest, of speaking directly from the ranks of the common people. Although there is no condescension in him, he speaks rather *for* the people. But he is high among the poets of social unrest because his voice was heard so far, and by so many. He was able to perform a difficult feat: to call widespread attention to the misery of the working class through a few lyrics. James Russell Lowell's lines are just:

> Here lies a Poet. Stranger, if to thee
> His claim to memory be obscure,
> If thou wouldst learn how truly great was he,
> Go, ask it of the poor.

Poetry like Hood's would have seemed a period to such as love not sorrow. But it was reserved for another than Hood to sound in verse the bitterest note of grief. It was Ebenezer Elliott who showed the nine circles of Hell entire. He puts into poetry with ruthless intensity feelings seldom found there. He does not so much blame the oppressor, as blaspheme, and as he writes, he seems to weep with despair. His rage is as mighty as Carlyle's, and it is touched with venom. Someone objected that he did not write like a gentleman. But Elliott made no truces with gentlemen, or, for that matter, with kings. His poetry is filled with invective, and reminds us of the stories of his speech-making. "They poisoned Socrates," he once shouted at a political meeting, "they crucified Jesus—*and they are starving YOU!*"

Ebenezer Elliott is the only poet in English literature who dared to make stump-speeches on Parnassus: his theme in poetry is not only the suffering of the poor, but legislation for them. He writes of the sliding scale in the heroic couplet; he sings of corn laws and Peterloo massacres; and his masters in poetry are Adam Smith, Jeremy Bentham, and Richard Cobden. In all nineteenth-century poetry there is hardly anything more strange than Elliott's wooing of the Muse. In boyhood he was a free trader, and in manhood a maniacal reformer, whose goal in life was the abolition of the food monopoly. His poems were bludgeons by which he intended to force this consummation.

He appeared suddenly as a poet in 1831. On March 19 of that year Lord Lytton wrote a letter to the *New Monthly Magazine* addressed to the Poet Laureate, Southey, concerning a remarkable poem by a mechanic. From this time on Englishmen encountered a series of poems dealing with the ideals and the wrongs of the workingman. *The Letter, The Exile, The Village Patriarch* (dedicated to Henry Brougham), *The Splendid Village, The Ranter,* with its description of the Chartist preacher, —all these lyrics, if such they may be called, were fierce diatribes on questions of politics.

There seems to be a good deal of Crabbe in Elliott, but it is obscured by his obsession for the issues of legislation. He often defeats his purpose by his own violence. He is so hot that his poetry often seems like melodrama, and even tends to border in its bitterness on farce. One lyric of Elliott's begins:

> My murdered baby! . . .
> Baby, forgive me! I forgive thy sire.
> O Heaven, forgive us both.

Others are merely verse renderings of maxims which Elliott had discovered in free-trade manuals. All are coloured by a sort of frenzy, and are heaped high with sarcasm, invective, and abuse. In *The Jacobin's Prayer* Elliott's invocation runs:

> Avenge the plundered poor, O Lord!
> But not with fire, but not with sword—
> Not as at Peterloo, they died
> Beneath the hoofs of coward pride.
> Avenge our rags, our chains, our sighs,
> The famine in our children's eyes!
>
> . . . . .
>
> Whip them, O Lord, with poverty!

Elliott's aim in verse was that of Carlyle in prose, of whom he is a kind of grotesque exaggeration: without mercy he denounced the inadequate "Morrison's Pill" legislation, so vehemently indeed as to amaze the masters of vituperation. Carlyle spoke of Elliott's troublous tears, and Kingsley accused him of deliberate savageness. Even Landor felt that another lion was abroad in the jungle, and commented with respect on the fury of this strange roaring. Nor was Elliott's voice in the slightest degree hollow; he was sincere. His models in poetry suggest his ideals for poetry: they were Milton, Otway in *Venice Preserved*, Burns, Byron in *Childe Harold*, Dryden, and Swift. His life was a protest against oppression of the poor, and he made poetry his chief means of remonstrance. In the preface to the *Corn Law Rhymes* he praises the union of poetry and politics!

The first effect upon a modern reader of Elliott's peculiar ideals is stunning. We seem to be present at a judgment of wrath and to be personally responsible. The heat of the man is overwhelming. He pours out the accumulated rancour of a lifetime.

> "I do not remember," he says, "the time when I was not dissatisfied with the condition of society. Without ever envying any man his wealth or power, I have always wondered why the strong oppress the weak."

Religious or philosophical explanations of life he waved aside. The theory of purification through suffering he thought a grim joke for those who had to be purified. Elliott lived in constitutional gloom. Whenever he spoke of an escape, during boyhood, from drowning, he was accustomed to add: "The more the pity."

> "I had also a taste," he remarks of his youth, "for the horrible—a passion, a rage for seeing the faces of the hanged or the drowned. Why, I know not; for they made my life a burden."

Elliott was an expert in the anatomy of human misery. There is much in all this to discredit his indignation. It has a personal origin, and is like that of the fanatic. But the fact is unchanged: his poetry helped to arouse England concerning social wrongs.

A final estimate of Elliott includes, aside from admiration for his fearlessness, something like pity for his warped conception of what the millennium was to be, and also amusement at his theories of poetry.

For the two great illusions of Elliott were that the repeal of the Corn Laws meant instant salvation, and that poetry was the instrument for the achievement of that end. His notion of heaven, I take it, was a field of untaxed grain, and his conception of poetry was a philippic against those who sought to tax such treasure hoards. Indeed, no title seemed to him more enviable than his own "C. L. R." Was he not known everywhere as the Corn Law Rhymer?

> "I have," he declares, "won my name as 'Rhymer of the Revolution,' and am prouder of that distinction than I should be if I were made Poet Laureate of England."

He regarded Carlyle as "the Homer of the age," and it may be that he considered himself its Demosthenes. "He is," says Alexander Smith in *Dreamthorp,* "Apollo with iron-dust on his face, wandering among the Sheffield knife-grinders."

Akin to Elliott in moods of despair, but without his virulence, is Thomas Cooper, "the last of the Chartists." Carlyle and Kingsley are often in the shadow of this sombre figure. Take down from the shelves (if you have the strength) *The Purgatory of Suicides,* a monstrous work of twelve volumes in Spenserian stanzas. The very fact that such a book was ever written is suggestive. There it is, a miracle of tedium and eccentricity, a long and futile anathema against priestcraft, bad government, and skepticism. Yet it is a memorial to poor Cooper, who himself drank the dregs of these evils.

"Indisputable traces," says Carlyle of the book, "of genius—a dark Titanic energy struggling there for which we hope there will be clearer daylight by-and-by."

Cooper was encouraged to write poetry for the people by Disraeli, Dickens, and Jerrold. He has little of the vigour of Elliott, but there is pathos in his abject hopelessness. One of his Chartist hymns, written in prison, begins:

> God of the earth, and sea, and sky,
> To Thee Thy mournful children cry;
> Didst Thou the blue that bends o'er all
> Spread for a general funeral pall?

> Sadness and gloom pervade the land;
> Death—famine—glare on either hand;
> Didst Thou plant earth upon the wave
> Only to form one general grave?

Hood, Elliott, and Cooper are but three of the poets who wrote for those who had no bread. There were many others, stout champions too, but they are nearly forgotten. Justly so. Yet to understand fully this aspect of nineteenth-century thought, we should glance into these. There is Charles Mackay with his hopes for a brotherhood of man; there is Eliza Cook dreaming of new worlds for the poor; there are various others. Fox, in his *Lectures Addressed Chiefly to the Working Classes,* praises for their aid of the poor in song Barry Cornwall, Joanna Baillie, Leigh Hunt, Thomas Moore, and Mrs. Adams. Everywhere in Victorian literature we stumble upon the poetry of the poor. In the unrest of the twentieth century nothing like this has occurred. The poor sing no longer, at least humbly or despairingly, of sorrows which seem irremediable. Their prose—for there is little poetry—is confident. Confident, and filled with precise claims—claims on the verge of fulfilment and always leading to more claims. The voice of the worker is different now from the voice which spoke through the poems of Thomas Hood, Ebenezer Elliott, and Thomas Cooper. He wears still the garb of Esau, but his voice is the voice of Jacob. Conservatives who are surprised at his presumption would do well to look into this verse. To the assurance of the present the road has been long and bitter; how long and how bitter may be appreciated by reading this poetry of social unrest.

Two Poems by Rossetti

Two Poems by Rossetti

The Blessed Damozel is now seventy-five years old, but she continues to hold her youth. She is still a school-girl's preference. She has been set to music by Debussy and been sung by the oratorio chorus of a woman's college. I have heard her chanted like "a carol, mournful, holy," at commencement parties of young ladies' seminaries. Older persons, too, sometimes speak of her sweetly. If one did not know Rossetti, he might infer from certain conversations that this poem was very touching, and was, possibly, written by the author of *Mary Had a Little Lamb*. If one betrays interest, he is sure to hear that the stars in her hair were seven; and more of the same sort, too, exact enough in quotation to suggest Mrs. Malaprop's echoes from *Hamlet*. I once heard the poem moaned (with surprising variants) by a lady who professed an unconquerable love for "the noble thoughts of poetry." She had it out in the gloaming of a Vermont piazza, and her listeners were powerless.

Among all Rossetti's poems *The Blessed Damozel* still seems to have popularity. One indication of this is that parodies of the poem keep appearing. The lady's immortality, however, is of rather a dubious quality. She enjoys much the same kind of vogue as Tennyson's *Crossing the Bar* or Longfellow's *The Wreck of the Hesperus*. She has won a reputation among the half-educated. American business men cherish versions of her in oil-paintings. I

have seen her in one of these leaning over the somewhat notorious gold bar flippantly, as from an air-
plane cock-pit. She seemed about to cast her lilies
at a New England sampler, which hung just below
her like a misplaced landing field. Her air was
buoyant, flirty. This time surely I "saw her
smile."

Has the twentieth century brought *The Blessed
Damozel* to this pass? This is a unique poem written
by a great Victorian poet. Yet it seems, in some
ways, to be the property of the Philistines. It has
assuredly suffered somewhat under their hands.
Other poems of Rossetti's—such as, for example, *The
Stream's Secret*—the popularizers do not care for;
they do not, in fact, quite understand them. Is this
true also of that hypothetical person, the general
reader? Have Rossetti's poems as a whole fallen
on evil days? Of all Rossetti's poetry possibly *The
House of Life* is the least neglected. I fancy that
many still read it, especially young poets, for certainly they bombard magazine editors with poems
obviously indebted for their form and tone to Rossetti's sonnet-sequence. The maker of modern poetry
does not, I believe, often read the poetry of Rossetti; he is too busy writing masterpieces of his own.
I fancy that he reads Tennyson and even Arnold
more than Rossetti. And the person we call the
general reader gets on quite well without Rossetti's
poetry, unless he is an enthusiast for the more
æsthetic types of poetry. So that the college student
is apt to have Rossetti for his very own. When

Rossetti is read now, he is usually one of a triune: himself, the teacher, and the class-room student.

Even then there is not always true understanding. The student is apt to be skeptical. The preponderance of the Latin strain in Rossetti he sometimes finds distasteful. I regret to say that he occasionally finds the sensuous poetry of Rossetti even a little comic. Imagine, for instance, teaching the "sick burthen of love" of *The Portrait* to an all-American half-back. Teaching Rossetti, even on brisk days, is likely to drape the room in a mauve mist. The ballads and some of the lyrics help to rarefy the atmosphere, but a fair interpretation of Rossetti's point of view does create a certain languor. It sometimes seems as if the "yellow 'nineties" were like a fresh breeze compared with the Rossetti 'eighties. One is reminded of Robert Nichols's picture of the æsthetic poet in gestation: purple hangings, dim candles, exotic fragrance, cigarettes of decadent Turkish:

"*I*," sneered a healthy intruder, "am going out to get some fresh air."

"Well," came the soft reply, "don't bring any of it back with you."

There are other aspects of Rossetti, but such a mood is in him; and it has injured him in the minds of many students.

Yet the thoughtful student does not dislike Rossetti primarily because he is at times redolent of tuberoses. He has another quarrel with him. He soon realizes that to call Rossetti "morbid" is as inadequate as any other popular truism about the Victorians. He learns that so to characterize him is to mistake an aspect for the whole. He becomes used to critics, like Hall Caine, who have shrouded Rossetti in sable. Thanks to them, the word Rossetti is an anagram for chloral, coffins, and outrageous beasts. What irritates most students is that Rossetti is relatively guiltless of *ideas*. They become resigned to long hair, and other idiosyncrasies in poets, but if they are studying the thought of the nineteenth century with a critical glance towards the twentieth, they do not forgive, at first, indifference to the age's trends of thought. "Rossetti may have kept a zebra and a wombat," a student once vouchsafed, amid applause from the class, "but he himself *was* an ostrich: he buried his head in Art!"

Many of us have begun a study of Rossetti by feeling like this. Few, however, have ended by dismissing Rossetti lightly as an æsthete. A study of Rossetti himself, and a thorough examination of the Pre-Raphaelite Movement are enough to prevent us from doing this. As the imagists keep reminding us, the point of view is the thing. Perhaps it is not wholly Rossetti's fault if we are not thrilled by such phrases as "brimming midnight," or "angel-greeted door." Æsthetically we may still be children. Browning's obscurity is excused on the ground that he possessed a superior intellect which would not trouble itself to be alphabetical in its expression. Something like this may be true of Rossetti's delicate register of æsthetic feeling. Possibly his poetry has unheard melodies and colours unseen. Swinburne thought so, and therefore worshipped Rossetti. Perhaps we should be humble about these matters. It is only a Carlyle among men of letters who can be cavalier about the secret realms of art. An open-minded attitude of wonder towards the subtleties of feeling in Rossetti may put us in the position of the person described, I think, by Turner, the person who objected because he could not see in a painting the colours admired by a friend. "Ah," said the other "don't you wish you could?" We do not like this sort of thing, but the realization that there may be feelings in Rossetti which we cannot understand— an attitude not unlike humility—is healthful.

For in the realm of subtle æsthetic feeling in poetry Rossetti, with the possible exception of Swinburne, is first. His more exotic poetry may seem quite unintelligible to our blunt intellects, but there can be no denial of his importance to English poetry on its colourful and emotional sides. Of course, his influence went to seed eventually in the work of O'Shaughnessy, Marzials, and poets still more shallow, but in the meantime it affected for good William Morris, and a host of other poets. His ideals were almost the standards of painting transferred to poetry. But their intensity definitely moulded the aims of later nineteenth-century poetry. This æstheticism of Rossetti's, this mastery of the arcana of esoteric emotion, made him causative. Because of him, it has been said, English poetry became more melodious, subtler in feeling, and more opulent in tone.

Rossetti was three-fourths Italian. Furthermore, he was an artist. The symbolism in his poetry is usually the symbolism of painting. For these, and for other reasons, much of his poetry is, as has been said, obscure. But there are a few poems which, if studied carefully, throw light on some of these mysteries. Two of these are in particular, I think, keys which unlock—not Rossetti's heart, but at least certain chambers in his mind. These two are *The Blessed Damozel,* this glibly-recited popular lyric, and a less familiar poem, *Jenny.* A student cannot do better than begin his study of Rossetti with these.

The Blessed Damozel has been called the most remarkable poem ever written by a boy of twenty. It has all of Rossetti's characteristic fervour, and in addition, a beautiful simplicity, hardly equalled, except in a few of his ballads, during later years, when the more ornate manner predominated in his poetry. It is charming in itself, but, besides, it tells us much of Rossetti. It is, for example, illustrative of principles which he was to initiate both in painting and in poetry. First there is the photographic realism in beautiful and artistic detail; for example, the three lilies and the seven stars. We do not forget these readily, and we see their counterparts in Morris and Swinburne. There is also the symbolism, as in the ungirt robe of the Virgin, an emblem which is to appear in many Pre-Raphaelite paintings and poems; in works of art so different as Rossetti's *Ecce*

Ancilla Domini and Holman Hunt's *The Light of the World.* Most of all there is the overtone of mysticism. Who can analyse precisely the emotion of the lover in heaven as he stands before the "shrine, occult, withheld, untrod"? Yet this is the mood we are to feel later in reading *Mary's Girlhood, The Day-dream,* or the *Venus Verticordia.* These are, in brief, the principles of the Pre-Raphaelites. But these young men had not yet formed the brotherhood. Obviously, then, we have in *The Blessed Damozel* confirmation of Rossetti's leadership in the Movement. Morris declared later how he had given up ideas of his own and had contented himself merely with trying to imitate Rossetti. When twenty years old, beginnings of the Pre-Raphaelite principles were already stirring in Rossetti's mind. The chief ideas of the Brotherhood were his. They developed, and broadened, but they exist in embryo in *The Blessed Damozel.* If we study the mysticism of this early poem, we are likely to be better attuned to the subtler variations of this mood in such a poem as *The Stream's Secret.*

In another way *The Blessed Damozel* illumines Rossetti's mind. It reveals an influence in his life which we must always remember in studying his poetry. Who is the damozel? What suggested this theme? That Rossetti had been reading Poe's *Raven* explains partly the origin of the poem. We have his own statement that he meant to reverse the situation described in the American poem. But was there another influence? Those who assure us that the lady was Rossetti's wife are rather beside the point. He had not yet met Miss Siddal. *The Blessed Damozel* is not autobiographical. But biographical the poem is, for the grief for the lost maiden is a reflex of the grief of Rossetti's master, Dante. "Albeit," Rossetti chants of the damozel, "to them she left, her day had counted as ten years." Rossetti is honouring no real maiden. Nor is he merely experimenting with a unique situation in poetic story. He is living over again the experience of Dante's sorrow for Beatrice. The note of longing for the lost maiden is heard frequently in Rossetti's poetry, in *Dante at Verona*, and in short lyrics. If we accept the influence of Dante as a determining influence on Rossetti, if we realize its importance in *The Blessed Damozel*, we comprehend more clearly the varied expressions of this influence in the later poetry.

Another characteristic point of view of Rossetti's is suggested, if less definitely, in *The Blessed Damozel*, by a minor detail, namely the heaven in which the damozel finds herself. It seems unfair to deduce too much from the picture of heaven given us in *The Blessed Damozel*, but indirectly Rossetti's peculiar conception hints at a basic attitude of his. It will be recalled that the lady does not care for heaven. This seems to be a pleasant place, but—there is no mistake—the lady is homesick. Like Aucassin, though for a different reason indeed, the damozel does not care for heaven. Heaven is impressive—and boring. Her one hope is reunion with her earthly

lover. In fact, apart from Rossetti's solemnity of
tone, the lady's heaven reminds us a little of an un-
congenial house-party. When the lover reaches
heaven, he is destined to "fear, haply, and be dumb."
As he learns the new songs of the angels, he will
have a very human experience: he will be em-
barrassed.

The truth is that Rossetti is not really thinking of
a next life, a life of the spirit, but a continuation of
this life, with its human emotions, and, in addition,
with certain disadvantages. By death lovers are
separated from each other, and, until both die, they
cannot be reunited. The whole conception is, of
course, fanciful, but if we read more of Rossetti we
see that this type of future life is about the only one
which interests him. Whenever he considers the
question, he regards it not as a thinker, but as an
artist, or poet. The essence of this heaven is its
literalness; it is a glorification of the more sensuous
aspects of this life. The lady's bosom warms the
gold bar. There are real hand-maidens whose names
are sweet symphonies. There are souls that are
flames, and prayers that rise up like clouds. Everything is actual. If Rossetti considers the next world,
it is always in terms of sense; he turns satisfied to
this, a twelfth-century heaven. For it is at bottom
a mediæval heaven, the heaven of the aureole, of
the Giver of Boons; an æsthetic version of the paradise of Thomas à Kempis. The lilies, the singing
spheres, the material resurrection,—this is the heaven

which both in *The Blessed Damozel* and in the later poetry moves Rossetti, mediævalist and romantic artist.

Of course we are not to forget that this is poetry, and that Rossetti did not believe that the purpose of poetry was to reflect ideas. This conception of heaven proves nothing about Rossetti's ideas on God or immortality. But it does point the way to a fact about Rossetti which should be kept in mind: that his attitude towards religion was chiefly artistic. In an age of scientific and religious upheaval he was equally indifferent to scientist or theologian. When on his death-bed he called, it is said, for the Last Sacrament, his friends regarded the act as a melodramatic caprice. None of this is indicated in *The Blessed Damozel,* but the poem is like an omen of his aloofness from the ideas of his era.

This, then, *The Blessed Damozel* does for the student: it suggests characteristic conceptions of Rossetti's. Of all these the most striking is the mood from which he is hardly ever free, that of mystical longing; that poignant and dreamy melancholy which springs from the origins of his poetical nature. It is most frequently concerned, as in *The Blessed Damozel,* with love and the haunting beauty of a woman. Here is, in *The Blessed Damozel,* for the first time, that strangely poised figure, all languor and tenderness; sensuous, yet reaching out to something beyond the senses. Sacredness invests her. She is enskied, made holy. Physical she is, yet spiritual; at once human and angelic.

194

Curiously enough, this quality of physical perfection as the symbol of spiritual beauty is the link with the other poem, *Jenny*. Curiously, for *Jenny* is a picture of a courtezan, and, although written within one year of *The Blessed Damozel*, it seems at first the antithesis of the earlier poem. But these ladies are, as we shall see, sisters.

"Vengeance of Jenny's case! Fie on her! Never name her, child!" Jenny is in truth seldom named in the best English literature. Unlike the French, our most gifted writers have not featured her. She has been depicted, with varying degrees of candour by Defoe, by Goldsmith, and by Clough, but she has never been a favourite heroine among us. She has, of course, secured a place in the drama. But in general we have been reticent about Jenny. "It is not," an English critic remarked, as if in defence, "that readers are shocked by such subjects, but that they are afraid they ought to be." It would seem that our restraint makes us veer from the truth whenever we do essay the subject. A Byron becomes cynical, or a Goldsmith becomes piously moral.

In *Jenny*, however, Rossetti offends neither good taste nor morals. Though he is playful, wondering, pitiful, he is never cynical. And though he is relentless in revealing Jenny's life, he is not revolting. Least of all does he ever breathe pious morality. The poem is an amazing composition of lightness without cynicism; realism without hardness; and tenderness without sentimentality. Swinburne's apogee is final: "Without a taint on it of anything

195

coarse or trivial, without shadow or suspicion of any facile or vulgar aim at a pathetic effect of a tragical or moral kind, it cleaves to absolute fact and reality closer than any common preacher or realist could come."

The reader likes Jenny. He likes the poem itself, but chiefly for the resemblance, which he feels, to *The Blessed Damozel.* For if he comes to Jenny fresh from the earlier poem, his memory is piqued. He is sure that something about Jenny reminds him of the damozel. A little thought clears up the mystery. Jenny, for one thing, is physically like the damozel. She has, too, the softly-poised figure, the long throat, the hair of "countless gold incomparable." But, more than this, she has the wistful reverie. It is not so much that Jenny resembles the damozel; it is rather that she is the same woman in another guise. It is the situation only which is different. One is sainted; the other debased; one blessed, the other unblest; one the object of worship, the other of lust. Both are incarnations of the poet-painter's ideal of beauty:

> Fair shines the gilded aureole
> In which our highest painters place
> Some living woman's simple face.
> And the stilled features thus descried
> As Jenny's long throat droops aside—

This is not the truism that writers tend to make their heroines of the same pattern. It is rather that Rossetti has but one type; that of rare, wistful beauty.

The law seems to extend throughout his poetry. In every poem the woman seems the same; only the attendant circumstances are varied. He can create only a lady of worship or a lady of dishonour: an Amelotte, or a Sister Helen; a Blessed Damozel or a Jenny. Christina Rossetti long ago wrote of her brother:

> One face looks out from all his canvasses,
> . . . A nameless girl,
> A saint, an angel.

What we learn, then, from the two poems, if we read them at the beginning of a study of Rossetti, is a truth connected with this favourite conception of womanhood: his belief in an ideal of physical womanly beauty as a symbol of the unseen beauty. We can, if we like, trace the idea back, in literature, to Plato, but in its perfection here it is peculiarly Rossetti's. In its languor, its intensity, and its abandon it is bound up in his racial inheritance; it is rather Italian than English. In the expression of this feeling Rossetti, in the later poems, wanders into worlds where we can follow him only with difficulty. This obscurity is found even in *The Blessed Damozel*. What does he mean precisely by the occult shrine? He is a mystic, and, though irreligious, is capable of tasting the sweet intolerable pain which a Crashaw feels. We may not have a personal liking for this, but we cannot help revering his worship of beauty, both seen and unseen. We see him exalted by the holiness and remoteness of the damozel. Or we see him saddened when, as in *Jenny,* this ideal is desecrated. As, before, his ecstasy was unbounded, so now his horror is without limit. As he thinks of Jenny's beauty and of her life, he cries out in pity: "It makes a goblin of the sun." But both in the joy and in the sorrow the central feeling is that of his ideal: beauty in woman as a symbol of the artist's ideal beauty. *The Blessed Damozel* has been popularized and has partly lost its significance, and *Jenny* is seldom read. But both poems are illuminative of the inner life of Rossetti.

George Brimley: *A Mid-Victorian Critic*

George Brimley: A Mid-Victorian Critic

IF you glance at the frontispiece of his *Essays,* you will be likely to call him a "mid-Victorian." He looks out at you, quietly austere, as if from his desk at Trinity College. He wears that extraordinary scarf of the 'fifties, and his beard—to modern eyes—is a scandal. The face is serious, kindly. Beneath the portrait is scrawled: "Truly yours, George Brimley." Who was he?

The dedication on the next page tells us that he was a friend of Frederick Denison Maurice. And a hasty survey of the chapter titles of the little green volume proves him to have been a critic of literature. This book is all that stands between George Brimley and oblivion. But it has done that at least. These essays are concerned with distinguished men of letters: Tennyson, Byron, Wordsworth, Patmore, Carlyle, Thackeray, Bulwer-Lytton, Dickens, Kingsley, John Wilson, and Comte. A humble book; but its essays, contributed to *Fraser's* and the *Spectator* in the 'fifties, have placed Brimley in the histories of English literature. In these he is always mentioned; and I have never known him to be mentioned without respect. "Had he been granted a longer life and better health," says Hugh Walker, "George Brimley . . . might have made a great name." Brimley was not a great critic, but the great critics are few. His position in English criticism is distinct and honourable.

That gentle—and orthodox—face suggests the mood of Brimley's life,—and of his criticism. It was a short life, only thirty-eight years; sheltered, but saddened by a terrible disease. He never wrote, so far as I know, a piece of creative literature. But he spent his life among books; handling them, reading them, and writing about them. Books were his work, his solace, his delight. There is little else to chronicle. His gentleness; his patience under suffering; his faith in accepted truths; his freedom from eccentricity;—these do not distinguish him from many others of his age. He was like many, too, in that he seems to have been unshaken by the subversive thought of his time.

> "I believe," says a friend, "he was an unusually good man, whose goodness was not always prominent to the ordinary observer, but who was, intrinsically, faithful, true, brave, and affectionate."

Brimley delighted in the peaceful contemplation of literature. In the essay on *Tennyson's Poems*, he writes of:

> ". . . those hours with cultivated and genial friends, in which the cares of the world are shaken off, and the best memories of the past, the noblest aspirations, the gentlest feelings, revive amid mountain and lake, for the votaries of ambition, science, or business."

If his picture and his biography persuade us that George Brimley may be conveniently classified as mid-Victorian, a reading of his book would probably rivet our conviction. His criticism is, first of all, moral. He believes that art should always teach us something. At times, his essays seem to be briefs for orthodoxy and the established religion; they might, we think, have received the imprimatur of any Christian bishop. This does not mean that Brimley is sanctimonious; he merely tests literature by the ways of righteousness.

This makes a difference. A moral point of view in criticism cannot take the place of disinterestedness, and its presence causes Brimley to be, sometimes, curious reading. The fault is obvious in *Tennyson's Poems,* his first essay. Brimley attacks the *Poems* of 1833 for their lack of ethical motive. A poet, we gather, who has Tennyson's noble ideals for human character, should be more careful. Brimley could not find the lesson of *The Lady of Shalott.* Its beauty, so he declared, only makes us "more angry that so much skill in presenting objects should be employed upon a subject that can only amuse the imagination." He manifests a solemn displeasure at Tennyson's early experiments in the lyric. *Fatima,* poor poem, had, he declared, neither beginning, middle, nor end. This is rather surprising. Who would like to see *Fatima* more Aristotelian? Or "airy, fairy Lilian" with a moral ending? Just here the browser in nineteenth-century criticism is likely to lay Brimley's book aside.

Criticism of this sort weighs down a large part of the essay on Tennyson. The lesson, he says, of *The Palace of Art* is imperfect,—a criticism which sent Mr. Saintsbury into a paroxysm. Tennyson has given us only "a *catalogue raisonnée,* richly illuminated." The interest of the poem should have been placed "upon the development of the law in operation." So, because there seems to be a moral purpose, Brimley thinks *The Gardener's Daughter* a perfect epithalamion. The following rhapsody is typical of Brimley when the mood of righteousness is on:

> "Mr. Tennyson's glory is to have portrayed passion with a feminine purity,—to have spiritualized the voluptuousness of the senses and the imagination by a manly reverence for woman's worth, and a clear intuition of 'the perfect law of liberty' through which the true humanity develops itself in the form and condition of an animal nature. He religiously observes the sanctities of love, and in graceful pictures"—

upholds the saints and the sacred traditions of the fathers, one almost adds in weariness. The trouble is that Brimley's sermons are monotonously alike. *Locksley Hall, Love and Duty, The Princess,*—all illustrate for Brimley "universal laws of life."

In the other essays Brimley continues to sound the loud timbrel of righteousness. He recognizes a hardness in Wordsworth's nature, but approves his moral purpose. This eulogy of Wordsworth might be placed, with changed names, in any hagiology, so worshipful is the critic's attitude. The study of Wordsworth is largely biographical, and some extreme tributes to the poet's personal life have an ironical sound now in these days of unsparing research by M. Legouis, and Professor Harper. The essay on *The Angel in the House* shows Brimley's moral tendency altered into something rich and strange,—strange at least for literary criticism. The paper has thirty-three pages. The poem under consideration is mentioned first on the twenty-ninth page, and sketchily described for the remaining four pages. The first twenty-eight pages praise the happiness of married life, and inveigh against triangle situations and betrothed couples. An engaging discussion, if you like, of the state ordained in man's innocency, but a top-heavy introduction to a review of four pages.

Brimley cannot get away from the moral point of view. In *Carlyle's Life of John Sterling,* the first of the briefer essays, he takes offence at Carlyle's emphasis upon Sterling's heterodoxy and he thumps Bulwer-Lytton roundly for falsely representing English social conditions. This is a severe arraignment from Brimley, usually so mild:

> "Dandy literature and superfine sensibilities are tokens and causes of a degenerate art and an emasculate morality; and among offenders in this way none has sinned more, or is of higher mark for a gibbet, than the author of *My Novel.*"

So Dickens and John Wilson, Brimley thinks, sacrifice too much to be entertaining, and Comte he places, naturally, in outer darkness. Indeed, Brimley is helpless before strongly original or speculative thought. He fancies that Byron's wild performance was designed by Providence to show mankind the folly of rebellion. And Comte shocks him so deeply that his reply is hardly sensible. He reverts not to logic, but to pious hope; to that which all our wishes bid us believe, but concerning which we know nothing:

> "If a practical test of the positive creed be wanted, there is one ready at hand. Let any one follow to the grave the wife, the child, the parent he has loved and lost, and seek to comfort himself by the reflection that the loved one is absorbed in the *grand être*—in the totality of organized life, life existing through all time in the universe. No!"

Brimley's emotion is noble, but it is not an answer to Comte. One can guess the reply of John Stuart Mill to logic of this kind.

Brimley seems characteristic of his period in still another way,—his manner of writing. The digression of twenty-eight pages in the essay on Patmore has been noticed. It makes one cry out in painful recognition: *"Fraser's!"* or *"The Edinburgh!"* Anyone who has read these periodicals has wondered about the connection between caption and contents. But Brimley's kinship with the popular style is more definite in his diction. The far-flung sentences; the array of words; the defensive tone,—these were commonplaces of the writing of the day. On the other hand, unlike the belligerent critics of the time, Brimley is too humble. Even when his judgment is most acute, he is apologetic. There is too little fight in him. He weakens his admirable defence of *Maud* by timidity in the face of the adjectives "morbid" and "hysterical." But, most of all, notice the elaborate manner, the phrase piled upon phrase. The curses of *Locksley Hall* are:

> "not the poisonous exhalations of a corrupted nature, but the thunder and lightning that clear the air of what is foul, the forces by which a loving and poetical mind, not yet calmed and strengthened by experience and general principles, repels unaccustomed outrage and wrong. With what a rich emotion he recalls his only recollections! Sea, sandy shore, and sky have been for him a perpetual fountain of beauty and joy, his youth a perpetual feast of imaginative knowledge and pictorial glory."

Here occurs a large section of the poem. Then more exclamations:

> "With what a touching air of tenderness and protection he watches the young girl whom he loves in secret, and whose paleness and thinness excite his pity as well as his hope. How rapturously—"

But I break off, like the reader, exhausted; there is still another page of this dithyrambic.

Elsewhere is a fusillade of nouns and adjectives to convey one fact,—that Wordsworth admired Desdemona:

> "In all that mighty symphony of maidenly admiration," Brimley remarks of Shakespeare, "of manly love, of stately age, of vigorous youth, of calm domestic peace, of 'the pride, pomp, circumstance of glorious war,' of

Studies in Victorian Literature

"boundless faith, of agonising jealousy, of wrath, hate, fondness, and despair, all blending into one complex devouring passion, he knew but the simple melody of the flute. In that woof of death . . . that marvellous and many-sided picture. . . ."

Is all this captious? Why should a respectable writer be pilloried many years after his work is done? Because it is important to notice that, in spite of these faults, George Brimley has a distinct place in English criticism. What I have to say in Brimley's behalf cannot counterbalance in mere space all that has been said of his faults: that he applies the moral test too frequently; that he is prolix and sentimental. But the defence outweighs the prosecution; it exhibits in Brimley a primary quality essential to a good critic.

This, even with all his "mid-Victorianism"! But before we examine this critical power it is well to modify our classification of Brimley. His faults were real enough. They are what we like to call "mid-Victorian" faults. Sometimes in reading of the 'fifties it seems that these were more obvious then than at any other period. And yet—last night I read an English review which was nothing if not "mid-Victorian." The truth is that these faults are of all time. I believe that I could point out some excellent Greeks, Romans, Elizabethans, and moderns who are "mid-Victorians," as we absurdly use the term. Brimley would have been Brimley, whatever the age.

His power lay in this: he penetrated with unusual insight into the enduring qualities of his contemporaries. It is noteworthy that all his criticisms dealt

208

with writers who are now receiving their real rating; he was concerned with the great Victorians. In almost every case, in spite of moral bias and verbiage, his verdict is that of posterity. In the babel of criticism in the 'fifties his was one of the few voices to speak the truth.

Take, for instance, *Tennyson's Poems,* Brimley's best essay. In the 'forties readers bought Tennyson's poems, but it must be remembered that many powerful critics were hostile. During these years Tennyson had a severe struggle for recognition. Carlyle and Fitzgerald wished that he had a "subject"; and Taine, in his *Histoire de la Littérature Anglaise,* was not wholly sympathetic. *Maud,* of which Brimley writes so discerningly, was especially unpopular among the reviewers. But Brimley tells his readers very definitely why Tennyson is great. We must forget Brimley's mannerisms and observe carefully what he says of the successive editions of the poems. It will then be found that his analysis of such a poem as *Mariana* is sympathetic and sound. Thus he says of the composed backgrounds in this lyric:

> "The minute enumeration of detail . . . is an excellence here, because no other means could so forcibly mark the isolation, the morbid sensitiveness, and the mind vacant of all but misery. . . . The landscape expresses the passion of the mind that contemplates it."

Brimley arrived at such judgments independently, and, when others were silent, he spoke out.

Brimley wrote as significantly of Wordsworth, although in the 'forties this poet was more firmly established than Tennyson. Wilson, among others, had proclaimed him, with Scott and Byron, one of the three great master-spirits of the day. Yet it was not many years since Jeffrey was saying: "This will never do"; when he was declaring that the *Ode on Intimations of Immortality* was illegible and unintelligible, and the *Ode to Duty* meaningless. What Jeffrey had said was still believed by many readers: that Wordsworth was guilty of childish language and mean incident. The influence of Brimley's essay on Wordsworth is difficult to measure; it was probably not widespread. But the credit is none the less Brimley's to have seen clearly and spoken wisely concerning a poet who even now is somewhat misunderstood.

Brimley's other judgments wear well. Who will quarrel with this passage on Thackeray?

> "*Esmond* will, we think, rank higher as a work of art than either *Vanity Fair,* or *Pendennis;* because the characters are of a higher type, and drawn with a greater finish, and the book is more of a complete whole: not that we anticipate for it anything like the popularity of the former of these two books, as it is altogether of a graver cast, the satire is not so pungent, the canvas is far less crowded, and the subject is distant and unfamiliar; and may be, its excellence will not help it to a very large public."

Moreover, on the art of criticism itself Brimley is curiously in advance of the other critics who preceded Matthew Arnold. This seems, indeed, like a premature word from Arnold himself on a favourite subject:

> "As to questions of form we have already stated that rhythm, metre, and all that constitutes the mode of expression rather than the substance . . . are spontaneous natural signs of a singer's emotion. . . . All, then, we have to ask ourselves in reference to the form of any particular poem is, whether it does so express the emotion of the writer, and what quality and degree of emotion it expresses—that of a great soul raised to the height of its subject, or of a little soul vainly striving to warm its thin blood, but puny, starved, and shivering, even in the presence of the central fires of the universe."

If Brimley is here abreast of Matthew Arnold, he is ahead of him in another judgment. He foresaw the immortality of Shelley. To appreciate Shelley's poetry is one thing; to tell why is another. It was Matthew Arnold's misfortune as a critic to fail signally in both regards: to find little in his poetry to admire, and to prophesy of him falsely. Arnold had no doubt that Byron would outlive Shelley, who was, he declared, incoherent. The understanding of the humbler critic went deeper. We shall leave our "mid-Victorian" with his tribute to Shelley, a tribute worthy in its fine flight of imagination, and in its truth, of any critic of the nineteenth century. It explains better than any single passage why Brimley will live as a critic of literature:

> "After the passions and the theories which supplied Shelley with the subject-matter of his poems have died

away and become mere matters of history, there will still remain a song, such as mortal man never sung before, of inarticulate rapture and of freezing pain,—of a blinding light of truth and a dazzling weight of glory, translated into English speech, as coloured as a painted window, as suggestive, as penetrating, as intense as music."

Newman's Literary Preferences

Newman's Literary Preferences

AT the outset of his *Life of Cardinal Newman* Mr. Wilfred Ward emphasizes the Cardinal's many-sidedness. To some he seems a religious philosopher, like Pascal; to others an ecclesiastical writer of history, like Bossuet; the casual student thinks of him as the leader of the Oxford Movement who turned Catholic, and later defended his "mighty mother" against Charles Kingsley's blundering Anglicanism; while the religious *savant* regards him as the most penetrating modern theologian. Today, unquestionably, all these aspects of Newman's genius still demand homage, but men read him now chiefly because, as Dean Stanley has said, he belongs "not to provincial dogma, but to the literature of all time."

Mr. Lewis Gates, in his brief but brilliant analysis of Newman as a writer of English prose, remarks especially upon his mediævalism:

> "Newman was intensely alive to the beauty and poetic charm of the life of the Middle Ages. One is sometimes tempted to describe him as a great mediæval ecclesiastic astray in the nineteenth century and heroically striving to remodel life in harmony with his temperamental needs."

The contention is sound. Mr. Gates had not space to develop his theory in his short preface. And Newman's close bond with Romanticism has never been adequately stated. His secular writings are not extensive, and students have not fully explored his

215

theological and controversial prose. It has been the fashion to catalogue Newman as "a great stylist," or "a modern prose-master," and then stop. But Newman was an apostle not only of two mighty churches, but also of that mysterious movement of thought and feeling called Romanticism.

One way of better comprehending this impulse in Newman is to understand more precisely his literary tastes. Much has been said of his attitude towards secular writing, but little of his pronounced preferences in English literature.

For to think of Newman as intellectually aloof from the world is absurd. His was the prodigious power of activity which has so often characterized great minds. He believed, as he was wont to say, that "life is for action." Anecdotes abound of his contact with the simple folk of everyday life. "Nothing was easier," says Father Ignatius Dudley Ryder, of the Oratory, "than to arouse Newman's interest, for everything interested him,—literature, politics, the trade and stipulations of the merchant, the circumstances of persons and places known to him; rural life; the studies of young men; the thoughts of the simple and lowly." Favourite lines of his, quoted in *The Idea of a University*, from Juvenal, suggest Newman himself:

"Quicquid agunt homines, votum, timor, ira, voluptas, Gaudia, discursus."

To fancy that this passion for life itself—for it was a passion, intense, comprehending, tender—

would not include an interest in the web that man has spun from his complex life, literature, would, again, be absurd. Though a colleague at the Oratory declared that Newman read with real attention only books which made for righteousness, Newman himself repeatedly avows his concern with all literature which his fellow-men had created. His conviction on this point often rises into ardour. He denounces in *The Idea of a University* the illusion of a Christian literature:

> "It is a contradiction in terms to attempt a sinless Literature of sinful man. . . . Give up the study of man, as such, if so it must be; but say you do so. Do not say you are studying him, his history, his mind and his heart, when you are studying something else. Man is a being of genius, passion, intellect, conscience, power. He exercises these various gifts in various ways, in great deeds, in great thoughts, in heroic acts, in hateful crimes. . . . He takes a thousand shapes, and undergoes a thousand fortunes. *Literature records them all to the life.*"

Every student of Newman's literary preferences should read carefully, entire, *The Idea of a University,* and especially the section in this book called *Literature.*

Regarding Newman's vast reading in ecclesiastical literature this essay makes but slight comment. He read and especially loved Saint John, Saint Chrysostom, and Tertullian, and there are countless instances of his devotion to Saint Basil, the two Gregories, and Saint Athanasius. Such study was vitally related to his conversion to Rome, and to his most constructive statements of faith, such as *An Essay on the Development of Christian Doctrine,* and the *Apologia,* as well as to his contributions to theological controversy in pamphlet, oration, and sermon. Classical literature, too, Newman made his own. Wherever the reader may travel in Newman's prose he will find the blessed realms of Homer, Euripides, and Vergil. For Newman delighted in imagery and allusion drawn from the Greek or from the Latin to complete the luminousness of his carefully developed thought. He admits, too, that in youth Gibbon's style fascinated him, but in only one case can definite proof of these influences on his style be named, and that one case is Cicero. Tully, Newman frankly acknowledged, had been, since early manhood, his guide and complete mentor in points of manner. Writing to the Reverend John Hayes on April 13, 1869, he says:

> "As to patterns for imitation, the only master of style I have ever had . . . is Cicero. I think I owe a great deal to him, and as far as I know to no one else. His great mastery of Latin is shown especially in his clearness."

Newman's brilliant essay on Cicero was written in 1824, and was republished in the first volume of *Historical Sketches.*

What we know of Newman's preferences in English literature written prior to 1800 is largely by inference. He speaks of reading in boyhood "some romance, Mrs. Radcliffe's or Miss Porter's"; at the

218

same time he read Tom Paine's tracts, Hume's *Essay on Miracles,* some of Voltaire. Evidently there was no systematic or even desultory devouring in youth of the literature of his own country. There exist few allusions to Shakespeare, or, in the Oxford years of reading, to contemporary poetry. Mr. J. C. Shairp notes that he once remarked to a friend at Oxford: "No! I was never soaked in Wordsworth, as some of my contemporaries were." It is safe to assume that he had no deep-rooted love for Shakespeare, although he discusses at various times Shakespeare's personality, his reputation, and his essential freedom from sensuality. But it is certain that he was able to quote regularly and freely from the plays, as he does in *The Church of the Fathers, The Last Years of St. Chrysostom, The Mission of St. Benedict,* and *Discussions and Arguments.*

Of other Elizabethan dramatists the echoes are few. But the prose-writers of the age Newman seems to have known well. Bacon is honoured with several pages in *The Idea of a University.* He was doubtless especially attracted by Bacon's style,—what he calls his "majestic gravity of phrase." For Bacon as a man of letters he apparently cared nothing; and his emotions towards him as a philosopher and a man were those of distaste and horror. To Newman Bacon was a heathen and a priest of the hated cult of worldly expediency:

"Alas, that he too, like Socrates or Seneca, must be stripped of his holy-day coat, which looks so fair, and

should be but a mockery; . . . and, for all his vast
abilities, should, in the littleness of his own moral being,
but typify the intellectual narrowness of his school!"

In a note on *The Idea of a University* Newman declares that he is in agreement with Macaulay's essay
on Bacon's philosophy; but that he concurs in more
than the general beneficent trend of Bacon's philosophy is inadmissible.

Newman's literary interests in the later seventeenth century were determined largely by his theological attitude. Concerning the Dissenter, Milton, he is silent. Himself an Evangelical in youth,
he doubtless understood Milton's attitude; his intellectual sympathy with dogma radically opposed to
his own was unbounded. Emotionally and morally,
however, there was but a slight bond between the
Puritan leader of the seventeenth century and the
Catholic prince of the nineteenth. The frequent
references to Milton in the *Apologia* are bound up
in theological discussion, but in his secular writings
Newman often has recourse to Milton's poetry.
"The world is all before it where to choose," an
adaptation of the fourth line from the end of *Paradise Lost,* occurs in *The Idea of a University,* and
everywhere reappear phrases from the minor poems.
On May 26, 1863, Newman writes Helen Church
of "the cheerful ring of the mower's scythe on the
lawn, which Milton long before me had noted." And
in *The Present Position of Catholics in England* the

indestructible prejudice of the Protestant is illustrated by the "day-star" in *Lycidas:*

> And tricks his beams, and with new-spangled ore
> Flames in the forehead of the morning sky.

Similarly, *Comus* is quoted in the passage on the Athenian Schools in *Rise and Progress of Universities;* in the same book Abelard's fate is illustrated by an excerpt from *Samson Agonistes;* and in the ornate lecture on the Tartars in *The Turks in Their Relation to Europe* the picture of Zengis or Timour on his throne calls to Newman's mind Milton's vision of Satan in state, as described in the first part of *Paradise Lost.*

Linked with Milton in Newman's study of theology is Jeremy Taylor, for whom Newman seems to have had something very like affection. *Holy Living and Holy Dying* influenced him perceptibly; one instance is a letter to his mother written on December 3, 1832. He urges her to proffer a heterodox friend "some book *on the Church* . . . like 'Thomas à Kempis,' or Taylor's *Holy Living.*" Altogether, it is difficult to ascribe to Newman much interest in the secular literature of the later seventeenth century. Of his acquaintance with poetry, other than Milton's, there is hardly a trace. Seventeenth-century lyrics which really move him are George Herbert's. Newman shared the Tractarians' love of Herbert. His highest compliment to Keble is to compare him to Herbert, and the death of his dear friend, J. W. Bowden, again moves him to thoughts of Herbert. On September 19, 1844, he writes Keble concerning Bowden's death:

> "Altogether it seems very much to realize George Herbert's notion of going from earth to Paradise, as from one room to another."

As Newman's reading in English literature of the seventeenth century had always an ecclesiastical bias, so his love of the classicists found fullest expression in the succeeding century. He felt, particularly, profound admiration for the perfection, within certain limits, of Joseph Addison's prose style. The resemblance of Addison's thought and manner of expression to Cicero's he considered striking. Cicero, he thought, would have done well in short essays, like those of the *Spectator,* if the manners or the age had allowed it. Above all, both Cicero and Addison, he believed, inspired their countrymen with literary taste. And at the end of the essay on Cicero he declares: "They resembled each other in the return [revived popularity] they experienced." Certainly, of all university men of the eighteenth century whose manner was especially typical of their age Newman would have named first "Addison, the son and brother of clergymen, the fellow of an Oxford Society, the resident of a College which still points to the walk which he planted." And, besides, Addison became to Newman, as he indicates in *The Idea of a University,* the supreme example of the folly of regarding literature as the precise product of a church,

222

a university, or a system. For, classicist as he was, Addison's immortality depends not on university or church, but on experience of life. Newman's apogee in *The Idea of a University* includes a rare tribute to Addison's place in the established body of literature:

> "The world he lived in made him and used him. While his writings educated his own generation, they have delineated it for all posterity after him."

Newman thought highly, too, of Doctor Johnson's classical erudition, but he showed no enthusiasm for what he wrote or what his character meant to the age. Moreover, he was unpleasantly affected by Johnson's hypochondriacal religion. A letter to the Reverend S. Rickards, written on February 9, 1835, has a passing reference to this: "In the last century Dr. Johnson is . . . [a] striking instance . . . [of] taking the gloomy side of religion." But he is able to quote with facility from Johnson in the disquisition on Cicero, and to allude glibly to Johnson's *mot*, as related by Boswell, that "the first Whig was the Devil."

— Newman did not care for the poetry of the eighteenth century. His allusions to it are negligible. Much of the Cardinal's theological anathema was directed against the negative philosophers and encyclopædists of the age; it is not surprising that he remained untouched by the poetry of Dryden, Pope, and their schools. In the chapter on the Macedonian schools in *Rise and Progress of Universities* he praises Dryden, and in *The Mission of St. Benedict* he creates a curious contrast to his own warmly tinted prose by quoting from the icy Pope. On the whole, however, expectation is fulfilled: he ignores the poetry of Queen Anne and of the earlier Georges.

More surprising, perhaps, is his neglect of the later poetry of the century. There is no evidence, it seems, that he was at all affected by Burns, Thomson, or, indeed, by any of the early Romanticists. Only one long reminiscence occurs of Cowper, but that is a moving and characteristic one.* On October 25, 1863, he writes Mrs. Brownlow concerning the popular false notion of the Catholic worship of images:

> "In England Catholics pray *before* images, not *to* them. . . . As to the nature of the feeling itself, and its absolute incongruity with any intellectual intention of addressing the image as an image, I think it is not difficult for any one with an ordinary human heart to understand it. Do we not love the pictures which we may have of friends departed? Will not a husband wear in his bosom and kiss the miniature of his wife? Cannot you fancy a man addressing himself to it, as if it were the reality? Think of Cowper's lines on his Mother's picture. 'Those lips are thine,' he says, 'thine own sweet smile I see'—and then 'Fancy shall steep me in Elysian reverie, a momentary dream *that thou art She.*' And then he goes on to the Picture, 'My Mother . . .'"

How like Newman! Self-revelation is here. Such

* Newman quotes from Cowper in *Loss and Gain.*

love of earthly poetry as this stern, tender man permitted himself was to be given to souls like Cowper's; never to the frosty complacence of the age of Dryden, but to his own peers, the poets of nineteenth-century Romanticism.

Father Ryder's brief record of Newman's literary preferences mentions no intimacy with his contemporaries in prose and verse, save through the medium of their books. Newman was a man of letters as well as a churchman, but he was never a member of a literary circle. Even Kingsley, his dearest enemy in literary dialectic, he never saw. And many others, it may be frankly stated, he did not wish to know. But for the writings of others he manifested the keenest sympathy and affection. These literary preferences are so distinct, so intense, and, when thoughtfully considered, so characteristic, that they illumine a lovely, and, I fear, an almost forgotten side of Newman's nature. Not now the theologian, nor the searcher of men's souls in dim St. Mary's, but an Englishman absorbed in the romance and beauty of English literature. We see him relaxed; *dégagé;* deep, as when an imaginative boy, in some old tale, as told by his beloved Southey or Sir Walter.

For the influence of Sir Walter Scott upon him was enormous. Among novelists he was interested, too, in Thackeray and Mrs. Gaskell, but Scott was, doubtless, linked with those mystical dreams of boyhood of which Newman was wont to make so much. In 1871, sending thanks for a copy of the *Life of Scott,* he writes:

"In one sense I deserve it; I have ever had such a devotion . . . to Walter Scott. As a boy, in the early summer mornings I read *Waverly* and *Guy Mannering* in bed when they first came out, before it was time to get up; and long before that—I think, when I was eight years old—I listened eagerly to *The Lay of the Last Minstrel,* which my mother and aunt were reading aloud."

Later Newman came to think of Scott's versification as slovenly, but he was deeply thankful for his power to turn the eyes of men again towards the Middle Ages, and he felt that in this respect he and Scott were basically in accord with each other. He came to associate Scott always with the idea of chivalrous honour. It is in the *Apologia* that this gratitude finds its fullest expression, in a passage which first appeared in the pages of the *British Critic:*

"The general need of something deeper and more attractive than what had offered itself elsewhere, may be considered to have led to his popularity; and by means of his popularity he reacted on his readers, stimulating their mental thirst, feeding their hopes, setting before them visions, which, when once seen, are not easily forgotten, and silently indoctrinating them with nobler ideas, which might afterwards be appealed to as first principles."

So in the pages of the ecclesiastic ring the melodies of the minstrel. Thus in the description of the persecution of the Christians in *Callista* Newman pauses suddenly to say:

226

"It would require . . . the magic pen of Sir Walter, to catalogue and to picture . . . the figures and groups of that most miserable procession."

And, as a single instance in *Loss and Gain:*

" 'Why, Fusby,' said Vincent, overhearing and coming up, 'you are like the three old crones in *The Bride of Lammermoor,* who wished to have the straiking of the Master of Ravenswood.' "

Nor is it fancy to detect the influence of Scott's genius for description in the novels of Newman. This is especially apparent in certain passages in *Callista,* such as the pictures of the plague of locusts, or Juba's madness. In Newman's lectures and letters, too, Scott is immanent. In *Discussions and Arguments,* for example, there is *Quentin Durward,* and in a letter to his mother, in 1820, we hear praise of *Ivanhoe.*

Unquestionably, Newman's liking for Scott's novels was intensified by the moral fibre he found in them and in their author's character. Again and again he praises their persuasive benevolence. As Father Ryder says, he thought of Scott's writings as "an influence for good as well as a source of artistic delight." On July 17, 1836, in praising Keble for an excellent sermon, he writes:

"You see it seems to me a great object, as Sir Walter Scott beat bad novels out of the field, in like manner to beat out bad sermons by supplying a more *real* style of sermon."

Studies in Victorian Literature

The continuance of personal respect and regard for Scott is evident in a letter written to Hope Scott on December 16, 1852:

> "When he was dying, I was saying prayers (whatever they were worth) for him, continually thinking of Keble's words: 'Think on the minstrel as ye kneel.'"

A modern reader will appreciate Newman's real devotion to romance for its own sake, if he realizes that next to Scott he loved best, in secular literature, Robert Southey. Southey he knew and respected, and he was fond of thinking that Southey's writings inculcated virtue. But, in addition, he read, re-read, and quoted, with pleasure, those interminable pæans of boredom, *Thalaba* and *The Curse of Kehama*. The reader of Newman's prose keeps encountering lines from these two poems. Charles Reading, the hero of *Loss and Gain*, on the brink of conversion to the Roman church, and speaking of the supposed corruption in the fold, says:

> ". . . I now believe it to be like those hideous forms which in fairy tales beset good knights, when they would force their way into some enchanted palace. Recollect the words in *Thalaba*, 'The talisman is *faith*.'"

In *Rise and Progress of Universities* Newman praises the massive learning in the two pseudo-epics, and in the *Apologia* Southey is mentioned in the same breath with Scott. Father Ryder says that Newman admitted having "an immense liking" for

Southey, and, in particular, for *Thalaba*. What attracted him was its romantic quality,

> "its succession of pictures, which so full of colour never glitter, have nothing of the impressionist about them; the tremendous catastrophe in which the hero dying achieves his victory, without early recompense."

Writers with a wholly alien point of view had, generally, little sway over Newman. Yet Thackeray, the novelist *par excellence* of this mortal life, was a favourite. Newman maintained his eager interest in Thackeray until the very end of Thackeray's life, reading every word that the novelist wrote, even to the last sad prose in the *Cornhill*. Thackeray's half-cynical analysis of life filled Newman with amazed pity, and from his quick taking-off he drew a lesson. Yet there is real affection in the letter that he wrote Miss Holmes just after Thackeray's death. He wishes, he says, "to express the piercing sorrow" that he feels at the loss:

> "You know I never saw him, but you have interested me in him, and one saw in his books the workings of his mind,—and he has died with such awful suddenness. A new work of his has been advertised, and I looked forward with pleasure to reading it, and now the drama of his life is closed, and he himself is the greatest instance of the text of which he was so full: '*Vanitas vanitatum, omnia vanitas.*' I wonder whether he has known his own decay, for decay I think there has been. I thought his last novel betrayed lassitude and exhaustion of mind, and he has lain by apparently for a year. . . . What a

229

world this is! How wretched they are who take it for their portion. Poor Thackeray! It seems but the other day since we became Catholics. Now all his renown has been since that—he has made his name, has been made much of, has been fêted, and has gone out."

Vanity Fair, Pendennis and the rest! Romance it is again that wins Newman. Thwarted romance, perhaps, in the lives of Becky Sharp and Laura, but none the less romance.

In fact, Newman's instinctive touchstone, in his reading, when it was not righteousness, was romance. It is, perhaps, just to say that Newman seldom cared for books whose general trend was not to make the will of God prevail. But it is equally true that there are notable cases of his liking books whose only appeal could have been their romance. A book which lacked both of these qualities could not hold him. Thus the realism and the agnosticism of George Eliot repelled him doubly; he could not endure the novels of natural fact. On the other hand, although he condemned Byron, he was unable to resist his ecstatic romance.

"I think," says Father Ryder, "he could have admired Byron heartily if his moral disapprobation had allowed him. I have heard him speak with enthusiasm of the third canto of *Childe Harold* with an '*O si sic omnia!*'"

In *Rise and Progress of Universities* Newman refers to Byron's *Bride of Abydos,* and various other allusions attest something more than acquaintance

with the poet. Yet, as may be guessed, Byron's way
of life received scant shrift from Newman. In the
Apologia he remarks that he has no sympathy with
the philosophy of Byron, and elsewhere he observes
that *Childe Harold* is a work of talent rather than
one of the highest poetical excellence. In his historical sketch, *The Conversion of Augustine*, occurs
his real judgment of Byron:

> "We have seen in our own day, in the case of a
> popular poet, an impressive instance of a great genius
> throwing off the fear of God, seeking for happiness in
> the creature, roaming unsatisfied from one object to
> another, breaking his soul upon itself, and bitterly con-
> fessing and imparting his wretchedness to all around
> him."

When, then, righteousness and romance are at
variance, righteousness conquers,—but there is also
that regretful *"O si sic omnia!"*

There is, too, a perfect and delightful consistency
in Newman's dislike of the realism of Jane Austen.
Speaking of Miss Austen he declares flatly that what
he expects in a novel is romance. Mrs. Mozley
quotes Newman's letter to her with his opinion of
Jane Austen with "a sense almost of disloyalty":

> "I have been reading *Emma*. Everything Miss Austen
> writes is clever, but I desiderate something. There is a
> want of *body* to the story. The action is frittered away
> in over-little things. There are some beautiful things
> in it. Emma herself is the most interesting to me of all
> her heroines. I feel kind to her whenever I think of

231

her. But Miss Austen has no romance—none at all.
. . . What vile creatures her parsons are! She has not
a dream of the high Catholic ἦθος."

An examination of Newman's literary preferences
is thus suggestive to those who regard Newman not
merely as an ecclesiastic but as a creator of English
literature. Such a study proves primarily that he
was a descendant of romantic tradition. Newman's
purely literary interests were not attached to the
seventeenth and eighteenth centuries; it is clear that
the emotions aroused in him by a Bacon or a Dryden
were chiefly those of amazement and intellectual
curiosity. Even a Shakespeare or a Milton was
alien to him in comparison with his profound and
instinctive concern for what was being thought and
written by his contemporaries. Two touchstones he
employed always and unconsciously: the love of
righteousness and the love of romance. Wordsworth's pantheism he disliked; the romantic strain in
him he loved, and he never tired of quoting the
opening lines of the *Ode on Intimations of Immortality*.* He liked Tennyson's *Mariana of the Moated
Grange*. Crabbe's realism he called "familiar vul-
garity," but he found delight in the romantic character of some of the *Tales of the Hall*. "This poem,
let me say, I read on its first publication, about thirty
years ago, with extreme delight, and have never lost
my love of it." Fouqué's *Romantic Tales* he praised,

---

* Newman was wont to speak of Wordsworth's "common-sense
humanity."

and *Sintram* engrossed him. A mental résumé of Newman's attitudes towards English literature of various periods and tendencies will convince the reader that, although never of any group, Newman was an integral part of the romantic revival. Possibly his isolation is but a further proof of the force of the movement; men so utterly different as Byron and Newman are moulded by its spirit. All that Newman truly loves in the writings of his contemporaries was allied with his sensitive feeling for the magic of romance. Every literary preference of Newman's proclaims him, directly or indirectly, a Romanticist.

Clough's Prose

Clough's Prose

MATTHEW ARNOLD once said that of all men whom
he had known Arthur Hugh Clough had impressed
him most deeply; a remark which has received
various interpretations. Some have thought it proof
enough of the academic cast of Arnold's mind;
natural, they say, for the school-inspector-poet to care
for this type of genius, so bookish, so introspective,
so essentially a product of the elder Arnold. Others
have conceived it to be a real assurance of Clough's
power; high praise from a high-minded and candid
critic. It is astonishing, certainly, to contrast this
simple tribute of Arnold's with his frank disregard
of other contemporaries,—especially Tennyson and
Swinburne. It was a fortunate comment. Because
of it we are inclined to study Clough more thoughtfully. And through its influence at least two of
Arnold's own poems, *The Scholar-Gipsy* and *Thyrsis*
take on new meaning.

"His piping took a troubled sound." So Arnold
describes Clough in *Thyrsis*. Clough was, he thinks,
a perplexed spirit. In writing the line Arnold was
thinking only of Clough's Oxford days. It describes,
nevertheless, the younger poet's entire life. The
troubled sounds never cease in Clough's poetry; they
are heard even in his last writings. In considering
Clough the mind turns instinctively to the ironical
Latest Decalogue or the despairing poems on *Easter
Day*. The latter are, indeed, heart-broken poems.
Much has been said to efface the impression that

Clough was unhappy. The biography written by Mrs. Clough,—still, in some ways, the best account of his life—stresses his workaday virtues: his cheerfulness, his humour, his contentment at home.

Clough's letters, relentlessly edited, reveal a lighter side. His adventures in America make delightful reading, and there is his mirthful *Bothie*. This may all be true. But in some fashion throughout the two score years which make up Clough's life the real man remains unchanged. The Clough of Rugby, the Clough of Oxford, the Clough of literature, the Clough of the half-dozen occupations which absorbed him,—these are the same, and basically they are the Clough of *Thyrsis* and of his own poems. He is, first and always, the doubter. "If," he writes while at Oxford, "I begin to think about God, there arise a thousand questions." And at the end of his life he says,—as if in the same letter—"Strive as I will, I am restricted, and grasp as I may, I can never hold the complete truth." Clough remained until his death a perplexed spirit.

Now it is precisely this hesitation in Clough which has endeared him to many. He has very human doubts about life, and he says so honestly. We recall his saying that he was like a straw in the draught of a chimney. The struggles of his sensitive spirit are reflected in his poems. On their title page might be written: the autobiography of a lover of truth. In these is recorded a search for truth, disinterested and unceasing. In these are his impatience with half-convictions, and his fearlessness. Matthew Arnold again describes him, this time unconsciously, when he speaks of the worshippers of the goddess Truth; Clough is not one of those who woo her so intensely that they bury their heads in the folds of her mantle; he is content if he may touch the hem of her garment:

> It fortifies my soul to know
> That, though I perish, Truth is so:
> That howsoe'er I stray and range,
> Whate'er I do, Thou dost not change.
> I steadier step when I recall
> That, if I slip, Thou dost not fall.

Clough's poetry, then, is admittedly the best source of a knowledge of his mind. From *Blank Misgivings*, written in 1841, to the poem at which he was at work during his last hours in Florence the story of Clough's believing heart and doubting head is found in his poetry. Naturally. Spiritual autobiographies may often be found in verse, more often indeed than in prose. But poetic confessions are likely to be incomplete. The essence is there, but the details are wanting. The reason lies in the character of poetry: it expresses the results of experience, ideas or moods, rather than the experience itself in process of development. On this principle rests the superiority, at least in one respect, of autobiographical prose over autobiographical verse; the superiority as a human document of, say, Newman's *Apologia* to his poems, intimate as these are. Autobiographical prose reveals not the crises of reflection and emotion, but the whole trend of thought as it grew. We see not halting-places on the road but the road itself. We find in Clough's poetry the record of his feelings; what we miss are the facts which occasioned these feelings.

Many processes of thought, for example, lie behind the lines just quoted, on Truth. And biographical facts throw light upon such a lyric as τὸ καλόν. A reader who stumbles upon Clough's poetry, knowing nothing of his life, is puzzled. Here is a poet, he thinks, who is sensitive to intellectual impressions; one who is sternly hopeful, or frankly despairing, or bitterly ironical. He learns that Clough pays allegiance in turn to the Greek poets, to positivism, and to various forms of Christianity. But the origin of these attitudes, their development, their relation to the currents of thought in which the poet's mind eddies round and round,—of these the reader learns little from the poetry. To understand fully Clough's experience he must turn to his prose.

As literature Clough's prose is nearly forgotten. There is little of it; including the *Letters* it would make only a fair-sized volume. Some of the brief papers were by their nature ephemeral: the speech on retrenchment at Oxford during the Irish famine of 1847; and *A Passage upon Oxford Studies*. Clough wrote literary criticism: *A Review of Mr. Newman's "The Soul"*; *On the Formation of Classical English*; *Lecture on the Poetry of Wordsworth*; and a *Review of Some Poems by Alexander Smith and Matthew Arnold*. In addition, he contributed to magazines the *Two Letters of Parepide-*

mus, casual exercises in speculative philosophy; *A Review of Recent Social Theories;* and the *Notes On the Religious Tradition.* This is all. Obviously, Clough was not a ready hand at prose.

If Clough had genius, it was for poetry. His prose is less inevitable, and never, like the lyrics, an outpouring of feelings or ideas. Much of it is laborious, and it lacks charm of manner. Its style is academic; the sentences are soundly built, but very clearly *built.* And their author is always conscious of himself, and of his reader. The literary criticism is done in a businesslike way, and is capable writing, nothing more. Clough had no real critical faculty, although an interesting collection might be made of his personal opinions on literature: Emerson, Carlyle, and Matthew Arnold are different because they "dip deep"; Mrs. Gaskell's *Ruth* is "too timid"; and Crabbe is "purely English in the Dutch manner." Clough's essay on Wordsworth is conventional, and by a curious irony he missed the significance of Arnold's first two volumes of poetry.

On the whole Clough's prose deserves to be forgotten,—except for our purpose now: its relation to his inmost thought. What do we learn from the prose? * Well, it shows us, first of all, that Clough was one of those unfortunates who are always estimating life without arriving at settled convictions. Clough was one who was destined to speculate; to yield to the good in a principle; then to see more clearly the evil in the principle, and withdraw. To be carried away intellectually again and again, and

241

then by the very activity of the intellect to destroy conviction, and revert to the original starting-point; introspection always, a lasting conclusion never." This was, if you like, weakness. At any rate his was an intellect speculative in its every operation; his was a mind tuned to all manner of truth, but one that fed upon itself, that watched its own processes over-carefully, and was too seldom swept away into unconsciousness of itself. In Clough's prose—especially in his letters—his balancing of speculations, one against the other, is always evident. Unfortunately the prose has been edited too carefully. In spite of the preface which declares that whatever "can throw light on the mind and character" of Clough has been given, we feel that we are reading fragments. However, the development of Clough's philosophy of life can be followed with advantage.

The story of Clough's boyhood is well-known. All the records of his life emphasize the influence of Thomas Arnold's training in conscience upon a mind already too sensitive to the exactions of duty. His experience in boyhood is suggested in *Dipsychus:* "I never fought at school"; but is really described in the poem's epilogue in which over-seriousness in boyhood is decried as a taint infecting manhood. Clough was not a normal boy. He was an athlete and had many friends, but one gathers that he needed a course in frivolity. When a man he wrote:

"Certainly, as a boy, I had less of boyish enjoyment of any kind whatever, either at home or at school, than

nine-tenths of boys, at any rate of boys who go to school,
college, and the like."

At Rugby during his last years he became a juvenile
Thomas Arnold. And when he went up to Oxford
he was wrestling with ethical problems which he
might better have reserved for his maturity.

Clough's letters written at Rugby are imbued with
this spirit. They are pious, altruistic, and filled with
worshipful allusion to Thomas Arnold. He enjoins
his younger brother George against indolence, and
beseeches him to keep close to God. Every letter
suggests a deep seriousness of attitude towards life.
One or two of the letters, indeed, escape priggishness
by only a hair's-breadth. We feel especially, in reading these letters, the sustained pitch of serious purpose:

> "I see . . .," he writes in 1835, "quite plainly that
> this [the departure of a friend] is far better for me,
> for now I shall not fag so much, as being of necessity
> thrown much more with other fellows, and wishing now
> most earnestly to know as many as possible; for there
> is a deal of evil springing up in the school, and it is
> to be feared that the tares will choke much of the
> wheat. There is a great deal of good in the top of the
> school, but then it is what may be called disagreeable
> good, having much evil mixed with it; especially in little
> matters . . . I am trying, if possible, to show them that
> good is not necessarily disagreeable, and that a Christian
> may be and is likely to be, a gentleman; and that he is
> surely much more than a gentleman."

The effects of an over-sensitive conscience begin to

243

show themselves even in school-days, for in a letter written about the same time there is a note of despondency: "I am afraid," he says, "that writing or thinking about these things does me harm."

Clough entered Oxford in 1837, and remained there eleven years. Many of the letters of this time are cheerful; they tell of friendships, vacation-parties, and travels abroad. But throughout them all recurs the mood familiar to the readers of Clough's poetry: the probing and testing of religious thought. These were the days of Newman, Pusey, Keble, Froude, Ward, and their allies and enemies. The controversy was hot, and Clough was in the midst of it. No one has ever declared with authority just how close Clough came to Tractarianism. It is unlikely that he was ever on the verge of joining the party. This he himself denies often, apparently with amusement at the notion. But that he was deeply interested in the Movement, even attracted by it, is certain. In 1838 he praises Newman's lectures on *The Mystical Power of the Sacraments*. In a letter written somewhat later he describes meeting "the heresiarch ἀυτοτατος namely, John Henry Newman." Although in another letter of about this time he alludes to "the Newmanitish phantasm," he details with sympathy Newman's views on Apostolic Succession. Going down to Rugby in 1839 Clough found that he "had been quite set down among theological gossips as a Newmanist." And in the following month he urges a friend—playful or not, the comment is significant—to hear the "Arch-Oxford-

Tractator" speak "on a topic doubtless interesting even to the remote barbarians in Van Diemen's Land." In a letter to J. P. Gell, written on October 8, 1843, he admits more than a possibility of his conversion: "I do not think I am particularly inclined to become a Puseyite, though it is very likely my Puseyite position may prevent my becoming anything else." This is not a blind embracing of the Anglo-Catholic faith. But it is not opposition, nor is it the distaste felt by many undergraduates at Oxford for Newmanism. Like all men, Clough felt the power of Newman, and characteristically perceived the good in his doctrines.

In the year of Newman's conversion to Rome Clough confessed a leaning in another direction. The *Life of Blanco White*, he writes, has almost

> "persuaded me to turn Unitarian, that is, for the moment; and even now I feel no common attraction towards the book and the party who have brought it out, viz., the high Unitarians."

Clough never quite weathered this storm; throughout the letters he praises at intervals the Unitarian creed. Yet during this same period Clough began to turn away from all forms of Christianity. The thousand questions about God upset not merely his orthodoxy, but his trust in historical Christianity. In 1844 he writes:

> "Without in the least denying Christianity, I feel little that I can call its power. Believing myself to be in my

245

unconscious creed in some shape or other an adherent of its doctrines, I keep within its pale; still, whether the spirit of the age, whose lacquey and flunkey I submit to be, will prove to be this kind or that kind, I can't the least say. Sometimes I have doubts whether it won't turn out to be no Christianity at all."

The following words to his sister show even more significantly the results of his self-analysis:

"I cannot feel sure that a man may not have all that is important in Christianity even if he does not so much as know that Jesus of Nazareth existed."

The tremendous change in Clough's point of view is most evident when these letters are compared with those to his brother, twelve years earlier; those in which he bids George Clough be constantly mindful of the living presence of Christ.

It is too much to say that Oxford wrought this change. Oxford was responsible only in part. Nor is Clough merely an example of a life of religious speculation. He is rather a unique instance of the effects of Thomas Arnold's doctrines upon a certain type of mind when this mind is subjected for a long time to another set of particular conditions. Many factors united to form the Clough who stands now as a kind of barometer of the disturbed religious thought of the 'forties and 'fifties: the sensitive boyhood, the moral teachings of Doctor Arnold, Clough's protracted stay at Oxford, and, by no means least, the peculiar character of that Oxford. This university has always been a seedplot for original thought. But never has speculative thought been more intense, more aggressive than in the Oxford of Newmanism. And never has such thought been taken more seriously by undergraduates and tutors. One of Newman's beliefs was that nothing was more important than for a man to arrive at the truth of religion, even to the smallest detail. Thus Charles Reading in *Loss and Gain* is indulging in no pleasant game of religious thought. What he thinks is recorded by the angels; it is a matter of the Day of Judgment; of life and death. Into the vortex of Newmanism and anti-Newmanism the susceptible Clough was plunged. What the result was the *Letters* show, even more clearly than the *Poems*.

When in 1848 Clough resigned his fellowship and left Oxford there is reason to think that his heart was light. A new period of more abundant life began. He travelled widely and lived for almost a year in America. Here he was honoured as "the *celebrated* author of the *Bothie*"; knew the Concord group; became a fast friend of Emerson and Charles Eliot Norton; and—strange climax!—was elected to Phi Beta Kappa. In England his position as a man of letters was at least respectable. Here he was generally accepted as a person, if not of genius, at least of great talent. His marriage was fortunate, and the tone of his life was happier than in the early years.

Yet in him, we may believe, was "still the old unquiet breast." Clough became a disciple of Carlyle, and Carlyle, he tells us, took him out into the wilderness and left him there. This was, as a matter of fact, the time when introspection and deep questioning ruled Clough most mercilessly. The difference between this and the other times seems to have been that his active outer life rescued him from depression. His speculation was not less earnest, as both the poetry and the prose show, but it was more detached, more resigned, less personal. The years had brought the inevitable philosophic mind, and Clough was able to reflect upon his own reflections, as Coleridge puts it, more dispassionately.

Although the reader of the letters written between 1848 and 1861 has an uncomfortable feeling that much has been excised, he continues to have glimpses of Clough's inner life. He encounters the same weather-vane mind with which he has become acquainted, veering in all directions, but fastened somehow on a firm base, that steadfast love of truth. Clough is interested in social reform, but cannot make up his mind concerning the best method. One day he writes a friend that he is in fact a Unitarian; on another he is strongly diverted towards Catholicism. "I was," he writes, "in a most Romanizing frame of mind yesterday. I was attracted to the spirituality of it." Mysticism allures, and at the same time frightens:

"To go along with it," he says, "even counter to fact and to reason may sometimes be tempting, though to do so would take me right away off the *terra firma* of practicable duty and business into the limbo of unrevealed things, the forbidden *terra incognita* of vague hopes and hypothetical aspirations."

At the same time his instinct for metaphysical thought is strong:

> "I am, I know, sometimes carried away into a world of abstraction when I write or study, or so forth. I believe my ambition also, such as I have . . . tends in that direction."

Again he admonishes himself:

> "I think I must have been getting into a little mysticism lately. It won't do; twice two are four, all the world over, and there's no harm in its being so; 'tisn't the devil's doing that it is; *il faut s'y soumettre,* and all right. Some of my companions are too much in the religiose vein to be always quite wholesome company."

The product of such states of mind is not likely to be action, and Clough often prods himself to substitute doing for thinking:

> "Let us not," he urges, "sit in a corner and mope, and think ourselves clever, for our comfort, while the room is full of dancing and cheerfulness. The sum of the whole matter is this: Whatsoever your hand findeth to do, do it without fiddle-faddling; for there is no experience, nor pleasure, nor pain, nor instruction, nor anything else in the grave whither thou goest. When you get to the end of this life, you won't find another ready-made, in which you can do without effort what you were meant to do with effort here."

Clough's poetry, especially *Dipsychus* and *Mari Magno,* deals much in painful analysis of common

human experience, and the prose has its share of this
dissecting habit of mind. Thus on marriage, the
theme of *Mari Magno,* he writes:

"The single life, according to the doctrines of compensation, has some superiorities, as, for example, that
of being more *painful,* which, in a state of things that
offers but little opportunity for elevated *action,* may be
considered a temptation to the aspiring temper. To live
in domestic comfort, toiling in some business not in
itself of any great use, merely for the sake of bread
for the household, does look at times a little ignoble, or
at any rate, unchivalrous. . . . What I looked forward
to originally . . . was unmarried poverty and literary
work."

So Clough's many moods come and go. His attitude towards God comes to be more and more acknowledgment of the element of truth in all creeds,
and adherence to none. A few lines written in the
latter part of his life, from which a sentence has
already been quoted, indicate the deepest conviction
he achieved, if conviction it may be called:

"I do believe that, strive as I will, I am restricted,
and grasp as I may, I can never hold the complete truth.
But that does not the least imply that I am justified in
shutting the eyes of my understanding to the facts of
science, or its ears to the criticisms of history, nor yet
in neglecting those pulsations of spiritual instinct which
come to me from association at one time with Unitarians,
at another with Calvinists, or again with Episcopalians
and Roman Catholics."

And for daily life he consecrates himself to work,

lightened by a somehow good. His belief in work is as intense as Carlyle's but happier. "All things," he says, "become clear to me by work more than by anything else." As to the other strain in him, hope, a dauntless hope in the face of fact,—this, we know, inspired some of his best writing. *Say Not the Struggle Nought Availeth* reflects a fundamental state of mind. So in a letter he says: "Go straight on . . . ," using a figure similar to that in the conclusion of the poem, "and one's sure to come out into a new country, on the other side the hills, sunny and bright."

This is commonplace enough. Clough's power lies in what is behind the resolute words. His determination to place truth first is based not on ignorance, or indifference, but on thoughtful rejection of the creeds that comfort men. Like a great scientist he had the courage to say that truth is better than profit. When he had cast off the guarantees of religion, Clough was still able to believe in action and in hope. He was able to "hope evermore and believe," as his refrain runs, not because he had decided anything about the baffling questions of life, but in spite of the fact that he had settled nothing whatever.

"I certainly am free to tell you," he writes, "that while I do fully think that the Christian religion is the best, or perhaps the only really good religion that has appeared, on the other hand, as to how it appeared, I see all possible doubt. . . . The whole origin of Christianity is lost in obscurity: if the facts are to be believed, it is simply on trust."

251

So he feels of any religion:

> "Turn the thing over as we will, we can't *make* sure;
> but doubt as we will about things in particular, we can,
> for the whole, *feel* sure."

This, then, is the value of Clough's prose, that we
have in more direct fashion than in his poetry his
study and his practical rejection of the creeds of his
day, together with his reliance upon a high and honest
hopefulness. It is doubt, yet faith; skepticism, yet
belief. All this is set forth in the prose. Each idea
has its expression also in the poetry, in such poems
as *The New Sinai, Say Not the Struggle Nought
Availeth, Alteram Partem,* or *Qua Cursum Ventus.*
But these should guide the student who is interested
in Clough's mind to the prose: to the *Letters,* and to
the frank confession written at the last, in the *Notes
on the Religious Tradition,* which bears as a text the
first stanzas of *Through a Glass Darkly.* In this
essay we find Clough's final word. Much of the
essay is in the mood so characteristic of him:

> "Lay not," he says, "your hand upon the veil of the
> inner sanctuary, to lift it up; go, thou proselyte of the
> gate, and do thy service where it is permitted thee. . . .
> When the veil is raised? . . . Who knows?"

Landor and His Contemporaries

Landor and His Contemporaries

SIDNEY COLVIN says that Landorians may be counted on the fingers of two hands. Few readers indeed know Landor well. Editors of magazines occasionally receive from unexpected sources enthusiastic estimates of the *Hellenics*. Needless to say, these are rejected. Students of the classics, if they are erudite enough, are sometimes devotees. But even these apostles of Landor are apt to be on the defensive. They base their praise of Landor on a few lyrics. Meanwhile others, with a taste for the picturesque anecdotes of literature, like to dwell on Landor's personality. These are fond of alluding to "the exiled Landor at Fiesole," or of referring to "Landor, who in a passion pitched his offending cook through the window into the flower-bed." (They sometimes omit the essence of the jest: Landor's reported exclamation, as he remembered his beloved flowers, "Good God, I forgot the violets!") They speak of the old Roman's *hauteur;* of his litigations in England and in Italy; and of his resemblance to Lawrence Boythorn in *Bleak House*.

Undoubtedly Landor has a tenuous hold on the modern reader. His prose is one of the curiosities of the nineteenth century. Most of us are over-whelmed by the *Imaginary Conversations*. To read them, or in them, means to feel uneducated. No school-boy learning will help us here. If we are not as much at home in the world of the ancients as in our own, there is little profit to be gained from turn-

255

ing the pages of these astounding volumes. The heroes of the dialogues come from the distant dead, where Southey boasted that he spent his days. They are as dusty as mummies of the first dynasty, although far more talkative: they bicker, denounce, and harangue. They are like ghosts on stilts. It does not matter that Miss Agnes Repplier implies, by denial, that modern dialogues owe something to the *Imaginary Conversations*. The fact remains that few read them today. Who in the last decade has performed the feat of reading them through, every word? Let such a person speak out boldly.

Nor is Landor's poetry read widely. The dramatic fragments and the epics are quite forgotten. To be sure *Rose Aylmer* and *A Fiesolan Idyl* are to be had in anthologies, and Swinburne has given his word that these shorter lyrics will be immortal. I have the word of a distinguished modern poet that these are constantly read even now by a few lovers of Landorian poetry. One must notice, too, the excellence of Landor, or even his supremacy in one particular form, the epigram. No one has ever used this ancient classic form in English literature so delicately as Landor. Yet, again, the truth is that Landor's poetry has a slight hold upon twentieth-century readers. They admit all these virtues in Landor, but they do not turn to him as they turn to certain other Victorian poets.

Moreover, our impression of Landor as a literary figure has become dim. Most readers of literature have heard of his eccentricities, but he does not live

in their minds distinctly as a man. In fact he sometimes seems hardly to belong to us. He is not, it is
now evident, one of those immortals whose books
pass, but whose personalities live on. He cannot,
for example, be compared as a dictator, as some
would have us think, with Doctor Johnson. For this
sort of immortality, something more is needed than
classical learning, a temper, and an ogre's laugh. No
groups will ever be formed for the study of "Landor
and His Circle." It is probable that Doctor Johnson
will be calling Boswell a fool, and will be stamping
his foot at Doctor Parr to the delight of yet unborn
readers; and that then very few people indeed will
be thrilled about the story of Landor throwing his
under-cooked pheasant into the fire. Landor had
those extremes of character which seem likely to
make a man remembered: uncompromising classi-
cism; fierce intolerance of the ordinary; domination
over other writers; and the loftiest ideals for poetry.
Nevertheless, his personality is not over-distinct today; hardly more so, I should say, than those of a
dozen other worthies of his time.

I have sometimes tried to sum up in a single word
the peculiarity in Landor's genius which has alienated
him from the modern reader. This is difficult to do,
but certainly one quality which has been a factor is
his aloofness. In his prose or poetry, or in his
personal relations, it is clear that Landor conceived
himself as superior. He wrote, he thought, for a
vulgar generation, and since we, too, are vulgar, we
also feel, I suppose, this condescension. To read

either his prose or his poetry is a somewhat chilling experience. Landor is like the oracle which prefaced its remarks by blasts of cool air. His manner of pronouncement is like that of Jove on Olympus. We sense often that he is wrong, but we do not dare argue the matter. He is inexorable. He does not advance an opinion. He issues an edict.

Nor is it so much that Landor is likely to be concerned with such topics as Lycophron as a poet, or the Greek word for violet, or that he speaks with such assurance. We are always forgiving learning in writers, and we are used to dogmatism. But Landor does not speak to us directly. He addresses us; talks down to us. He cannot stir our feelings. His notions on life may be true, but we receive them without enthusiasm. I suppose the real reason for this is that Landor's writings reflect not his ideas on life, but those he has culled from books. His ideas echo in our own experience, but somewhere on the way to us his emotion has been frozen. To recognize our feelings done in marble, we should read Landor's apothegms. The curt Hazlitt is not an exuberant writer, but passages from his essay *On the Fear of Death* are glowing when compared with Landor's frequent speculations on the same subject. The following from the *Pentameron* is characteristic:

> "Death can only take away the sorrowful from our affections; the flower expands; the colorless film that enveloped it falls off and perishes. . . . Would we break a precious vase, because it is as capable of containing the bitter as the sweet? No: the very things which

touch us the most sensibly are those which we should be the most reluctant to forget. The noble mansion is most distinguished by the beautiful images it retains of beings past away; and so is the noble mind. The damps of autumn sink into the leaves and prepare them for the necessity of their fall: and thus insensibly are we, as years close round us, detached from our tenacity of life by the gentle pressure of recorded sorrows."

More than all else it is this aloofness which makes Landor an unpopular writer today.

But the weaknesses of Landor's writings and personality are not a discovery of our own time. There was no mystery in Landor's life. His contemporaries were sensible of this aloofness. Why, then, was his influence so marked during the early decades of the nineteenth century? Why did Southey, Shelley, Browning, and Swinburne think him not merely great but among the greatest of his era?

In answer it may, of course, be said that such a person as Landor and such writings as his would affect contemporaries more than posterity. They had a novelty which, viewed at first hand, would attract attention. We are more cynical than that earlier generation about strangeness in literature. Perhaps Landor, if alive, would not arouse the interest now that he did in the first half of the nineteenth century. Modern psychology has taught us not to be surprised at the most eccentric temperament. The biologists or the neurologists can explain anyone, or anything. In one way it would be rather pleasant to have Landor, like some other geniuses of the past, alive. What a pleasure to have him psycho-analysed! Although the force of Landor's personality is now somewhat spent, it was natural that literary men should have felt then that the aloofness, now a wall about him, hid a mighty genius. It was not peculiar that for a time he was regarded as a kind of demi-god of literature. But more precisely there was a real reason for his influence upon men of letters. What that was we should try to determine. It re-solves itself finally, I think, into Landor's ideal of life, and so of literature.

Unquestionably Landor's prose consolidated his reputation. Mr. Howitt remarks that "his *Ima-ginary Conversations* have eclipsed his verse." This may be true. But eclipses are temporary phenomena. Certainly the *Conversations* did not win the esteem of Shelley, or Swinburne. They were concerned with his poetry. As the *Imaginary Conversations* ap-peared in ever-increasing numbers, they excited re-spect for Landor's learning, but in all the gossip of the period, there is no evidence that they moved writers deeply, or that they were regarded as the chief source of his influence. Most readers thought of them simply as mausoleums of learning. They stimu-lated some discussion, for they were filled with eccen-tric comments on all phases of life: economics, politics, religion, and literature; but most seekers after truth were lost in a labyrinth of learning, for which Landor's pompous manner was an imperfect guide. The style of the *Conversations* was itself terrifying. "He has never learned," says Coleridge, "how to write simple and lucid English."

Landor and His Contemporaries

Much might be said of Landor's didactic treatment of the subjects just mentioned, or of his attitude towards history, ethics, and manners. For students of literature Landor's vagaries are most striking whenever he speaks of literature. He was famous for his odd critical opinions of books. We meet with these everywhere in the prose, opinions far less effective, it must be admitted, in his writings than in his talk; opinions such as Landor loved to deliver, with hyperbole and laughter, to those who sat about him in the "villa Landora" in Fiesole. He judged, says Edward Fitzgerald, "with a most compromising perversity which the Phrenologists must explain to us after his Death." Leslie Stephen sums up the matter in his brief biography of Landor:

> "Even in literature," he says, "his criticisms, though often admirably perceptive, are too often wayward and unsatisfactory, because at the mercy of his prejudices. He idolized Milton, but the mediævalism of Dante dimmed his perception of Dante's great qualities. Almost alone among poets he always found Spenser a bore."

Nineteenth-century reminiscences reflect Landor's capricious literary judgments. Henry Crabb Robinson, for example, relates how Landor maintained

> "Blake to be the greatest of poets; that Milnes is the greatest poet now living in England; and that Scott's *Marmion* is superior to all that Byron and Wordsworth have written, and the description of the battle better than anything in Homer. . . ."

261

Literary criticism is not the staple of the *Imaginary Conversations,* but it is typical, in its oddity, of what the average reader found there. He did not care for the stern pictures of antiquity, the heavy argument, the stately, involved sentences.

Yet in the *Imaginary Conversations* and in the other prose, if the reader is attentive, may be found that ideal of life and literature which affected Landor's contemporaries. What that was, however, may be best conceived in connection with his poetry, and in reference to his personality. The influence of his poetry upon the ordinary reader, like that of the prose, was slight. The narrative poems, and even the lyrics won over only a small audience. Landor founded no school, nor had he, like other nineteenth-century poets, a group of imitators. The younger poets copied Wordsworth and Tennyson and Rossetti, but, save, perhaps, Swinburne, it did not occur to them to copy Landor,—any more than to copy Pindar! Classical imitations had become a hobby, but Landor was inimitable both in his obscure themes and in his austere manner. Compared with his the classical poems of Tennyson or Arnold were like pleasant fairy-tales of Greece.

But if the current of influence upon contemporary poets was narrow, it was also deep. Imitators were rare, but worshippers were plentiful. And the noteworthy fact is that these worshippers were the great writers. Thus Shelley read Landor unceasingly. Lamb, drunk or sober, was forever quoting *Rose Aylmer;* and Southey's adulation was fantastic.

Tribute follows tribute. Of *Count Julian* he wrote that no drama to which it can be compared had ever yet been written, except it were by the same hand. Southey shaped *Thalaba* upon the scheme of *Gebir,* and he dedicated to Landor his *Curse of Kehama.* Possibly, we think, Southey's judgment was impaired by his friendship for Landor. But Shelley, who had no such attachment, could not let *Gebir* alone. His biographer, Hogg, tells the story. He often found Shelley reading *Gebir.* There was something in that poem which caught his fancy. He would read it aloud, or to himself, with a tiresome pertinacity. One morning Hogg went to his rooms to tell him something of importance, but he would attend to nothing but *Gebir.* And years later Swinburne bows down to *Count Julian.* It is, he says,

> "the sublimest poem published in our language between the last masterpiece of Milton and the first masterpiece of Shelley. . . . No comparable work is to be found in English poetry between the date of *Samson Agonistes* and the date of *Prometheus Unbound.*"

And as spokesman for the prose-writers, De Quincey declares that *Gebir* is no less than "Æschylean." Thus the influence of Landor's poetry is not only real, but it is directed towards the best minds of his generation.

Now, it is clear that what stirred these poets to admiration was Landor's ideal for poetry. Everyone knows what this was. He abhorred the facile, the commonplace, and the sensational. He proclaimed by precept and by the example of his own poetry that the desirable qualities of poetry were restraint in form and feeling; dignity of manner; and a kind of austere emotion. His models were, of course, though he himself is often more like the Romans, Greek. His poetry was moulded upon an instinctive ideal of τὸ καλόν in literature. The ideal is also apparent in the prose. But the prose does not reveal as does the poetry certain graces of feeling and manner. No one would guess that the author of the *Imaginary Conversations* could write of flowers, as Landor does, in *A Fiesolan Idyl*. The poetry shows the gentler side of his nature. "He is," says Leigh Hunt, "like a strong mountain-pine that should produce lilies." In the poetry is Landor's severity of mood towards life as a whole, but also his tenderness for youth, for children, for flowers. And every line of this poetry is written with that high dignity which Landor thought inseparable from true poetry. Shelley and Browning did not imitate these qualities. No one could do that. But it is not surprising that they felt their power. Moreover, Landor's poetry has a splendid consistency. He never drops the rôle of the poet who writes for the few. In fact, it is not a rôle at all; it is merely himself, "by the grace of God, Walter Savage Landor."

Because Landor's ideals for literature were definite, because they were unflinching, he profoundly affected his contemporaries. The influence has not lived on, for fairly obvious reasons, into our own time. But no one can question the vitality of the influence in his own era. This influence was enforced by his personality. The aloofness of mind found its expression in his poetry in his seriousness of manner. In ordinary life it manifested itself in a stormy domination of everyone whom he knew. In poetry it was passive; he ignored the tastes of the vulgar. But in real life—after all, it was quite a natural reaction—it was aggressive; he actively abused the commonplace. His success in domineering came from his picturesque individuality. He was fitted by nature for the part of an angry lion. There was a certain magnificence about Landor. Not everyone could become famous throughout Europe for litigation, quarrels, and violence of temper, and yet seem to be kingly. Yet Landor did this. His explosive temper somehow drove home the lessons suggested by his poetry, that the only ideal for literature worth maintaining is that of high contempt for anything except the lofty, the dignified, and the austere.

Thus the contrast between the calm of his poetry and the turbulence of his everyday life is less of a paradox than it seems. Both attitudes are protests against commonplaceness in life and literature. As we reconstruct Landor's personality and study his ideals for literature, it is easy to understand the influence he had personally upon his contemporaries. Extreme eccentricity, like extreme ugliness, may become an asset instead of a liability. Had Landor's temper been as unruffled as his poetry, Fiesole would not have been such a Mecca for literary men. Here was this venerable Prometheus of literature, stealing for nearly a century his fire from heaven, writing literally the style of gods, laughing at his fellow-poets endlessly, scorning them, and pronouncing unreasonable, but strangely stimulating opinions on literature and life. Here he was, loving Fiesole, but longing for England. Here he remained, cast out of England, white haired, titanic, a kind of unregenerate King Lear. Pomero, most insolent of literary dogs, sat on the poet's head, looking down towards Florence, thinking doubtless, like his master, of the commonplaceness of the human race: *"Il vecchio con quel bel canino!"* There were, Landor remarked to Parr, probably thirty people in the world who could not be described by the adjective "vulgar."

There is hardly a poet or prose-writer of the nineteenth century who has not recorded an impression of this strange personality. Landor became almost a national figure. John Sterling declared that he had recognized Landor in a coach from the resemblance his conversation bore to that of his characters in the *Imaginary Conversations*. Dickens made him known to countless readers, and, far from being displeased with the caricature, Landor confessed that he liked it. Naturally, so extraordinary a person did not escape an etching by Thomas Carlyle:

"A tall, broad, burly man," he writes Emerson, who revered Landor, "with gray hair, and large fierce-rolling eyes; of the most restless, impetuous vivacity, not to be held in by the most perfect breeding, expressing itself in high-colored superlatives, indeed in reckless exaggerations, now and then in a dry, sharp laugh not of sport but of mockery; a wild man whom no extent of culture had been able to tame!"

Carlyle dines with Landor, and notes in his *Journal:*

"A proud, irascible, trenchant, yet generous, veracious, and very dignified old man; quite a ducal or royal man in the temper of him; reminded me something of old Sterling, except that for that Irish blarney, you must substitute a fund of Welsh choler."

To answer the initial question about the reason for Landor's appeal to his own generation, we must examine still further the reactions to his personality. They are not difficult to find; in fact they are everywhere. In the main his temper and independence attracted rather than antagonized. Men could not help listening to "that deep-mouth'd Bœotian 'Savage Landor,'" as Byron called him in *Don Juan*. He did, however, anger some. It was natural that the peppery Hazlitt should find Landor arrogant and capricious. Mrs. Browning was inclined to be offended at his insolence. When Browning was not the object of his spleen, she thought him admirable, but at other times she analysed him resentfully:

"Is it not true," she wrote her husband, "that Landor . . . is one of the men who carry their passions about with them into everything, as a boy would pebbles . . . muddying every clear water, with a stone here and a stone there? The end is, that we lose the image of himself in the serene depth, as we might have had it— and the little stone comes to stand for him. How unworthy of such a man as Landor, such weakness is!

267

To *think* with one's temper! One might as well be at once Don Quixote, and fight with a warming pan."

Usually, however, it is not Landor's temper, but his judgment that is thought Quixotic. On this point Leslie Stephen's opinion has been quoted. There is a story, perhaps apocryphal, about Landor's behaviour when Mrs. Browning sent him Lytton's *Lucile:* "Who could ever," he cried, "read a poem which began with *But?*" Later he adds: "Why, God bless my soul, it's the finest thing I ever read in my life." Caroline Fox tells a tale of whimsical criticisms offered by Landor to Archdeacon Hare:

"The only well-drawn figure in existence [is] a female by Overbeck in his picture of 'Children Brought to Christ'; Milton wrote one good line, but he forgot it; Dante perhaps six, his description of Francesca; Carlyle's *French Revolution,* a wicked book, he had worn out one volume in tossing onto the floor at startling passages."

"His old age," concludes Miss Fox, "is an amalgam of the grotesque and forlorn." And Carlyle, who loved conversation, declared that Landor talked him into a syncope.

All this thrown off in the midst of volleys of laughter! Coleridge's sing-song voice and Lamb's stutter are not so vivid in Victorian gossip as Landor's laughter.

"I found in him," writes Tom Moore, "all the air and laugh of a hearty country gentleman."

"His laugh is in peals, and climbing," says Leigh
Hunt, "he seems to fetch every fresh one from a higher
story."

This laughter amazed Wordsworth and terrified
Mrs. Browning:

"The crushing throat peals of Mr. Landor's laughter.
He laughs . . . like an ogre—he laughs as if laughter
could kill and he knew it, thinking of an enemy."

To this literary giant, dwelling aloof on the hills
above Florence among his books and pictures came,
in humble worship, "the youngest to the oldest
singer,"—Swinburne. Landor saw a fiery head
bowed before him. Such frank homage was 'disconcerting, even to Landor. Yet he could hardly take
offence, and a real friendship sprang up between
them. Soon Landor was presenting Swinburne with
a Correggio (he thought it was one) and was shout-
ing, so the story goes, in response to the young poet's
demurral: "By God! You shall take it!"

That Landor should have interested his contemporaries is not surprising. The significant thing is
that he became in literature a constructive force. In
spite of insane literary verdicts, Landor's praise of
new books was eagerly desired. He is, Southey said,
"the only man living of whose praise I was ambitious,
or whose censure would have humbled me." And
Robert Browning wrote to Mrs. Browning: "Lan-
'dor's praise is altogether a different gift; a gold vase
from King Hiram."

The very waywardness and intensity of Landor's conversations seem to have been his strength. Miss Kate Field in her remarkable picture of Landor as a man says:

> "It was impossible to be in Landor's society a half hour and not reap advantage. His great learning, varied information, extensive acquaintance with the world's celebrities, ready wit, and even readier repartee, rendered his conversation wonderfully entertaining."

And Milnes, after paying tribute to Landor's writings, adds:

> "It was his conversation that left . . . the most delightful and permanent impression; so affluent, animated, and coloured; so rich in knowledge and illustration; so gay and yet so weighty—such bitter irony and such lofty praise uttered with a voice fibrous in all its tones, whether gentle or fierce—it equalled, if not surpassed, all that has been related of the table talk of men eminent for social speech."

And we have also Mrs. Browning's crowning tribute:

> "Robert always said that he owed more as a writer to Landor than to any contemporary."

Today much of Landor's conversation seems like rhodomontade, and his domineering a pose. But Landor was sincere. He was quaintly heroic, and heroics were for him natural. Southey wrote to John Rickman:

"He is more than any of the gods of all my mythologies, for his very words are thunder and lightning,—such is the power and splendour with which they burst out: but all is perfectly natural, there is no trick about him,—no preaching, no parade, no playing off."

So in the renewed study of Victorian literature it is well to notice the special gifts of Walter Savage Landor, and reflect on the particular task which he performed. Such an appraisal must begin, it seems to me, with the realization that nothing new can be expected of Landor's influence now or hereafter. His work is finished. Soon his devotees may be counted on the fingers of *one* hand. In 1890 W. B. Clymer wrote of Landor's poetry:

"Its chance in the struggle for existence rests on the likelihood of there being in future generations a few men with Emerson's unjaded taste for 'pure literature.'"

Perhaps. "Pure learning" would be nearer the truth. Margaret Oliphant may speak of *Count Julian* as "worthy of the hand which showed us Hamlet and Othello." Stedman may compare *Gebir* to Keats's *Hyperion*. But Miss Mitford is nearer fact when she speaks, with curious juxtaposition, of out-of-the-way writers like Colley Cibber, and W. S. Landor. The tendency is to think of Landor even as a minor figure.

Minor he is now, but minor in his own day he was not. It is difficult to state in a few words the exact character of Landor's influence among his contemporaries. It was exerted upon a few through his poetry, and upon many more through his personality. Certainly its essence lay in his austere idealism. In an age in which poets were introspective, Landor was objective. When others were expressing moods of unrest, reflecting the confused thought of the century, Landor was calmly imitating Pindar. When others were exhibiting their wounded feelings, Landor was concerned in his poetry with subtle and delicate emotional values,—most of them Greek in origin. Landor never relinquished the ideal that poetry should be restrained, intellectual, and architectonic. Such an ideal had its effect. Landor had an ennobling influence upon the few poets whom he inspired.

"Consider," says Stedman, "the names of those who, having met him and known his works, perceive in him something great and worshipful."

The Parent of School-Boy Novels

The Parent of School-Boy Novels

A HISTORIAN of literature has remarked that the three most popular books of boys of fifteen or fifty are *Robinson Crusoe, Treasure Island,* and *School-Days at Rugby.* In all strictness the first two masterpieces are endemic to a slightly earlier period of boyhood. At the age of ten every boy, unless there is something the matter with him, wishes ardently to become a pirate. It is then that he reads about Man Friday or the epic of John Silver. But at fifteen has come disillusionment. The chances of being either pirate or president seem less brilliant. And now, instead of the South Seas, another heaven beckons him on, the Valhalla of boy-heroes—school with football and baseball fields, the river, and the friendships of youth. He feels the lure, as Carlyle puts it, of "manifold collision and communication of . . , young souls." Who that has known its romance can forget it? The real boy of fifty never does, and he reads the novels of school-boy life as eagerly as his sons. For all who have known youth they have an enduring charm.

At this very moment they fall from the press like the proverbial leaves of Vallombrosa. A Princeton writer's story is in its eighth reprint; and the silent majority of its readers are the boys known as college alumni. The circulation of an American periodical overflowed its bounds recently when it published Owen Johnson's Lawrenceville stories. Seventy thousand people in a bowl or a stadium indicate one positive American interest. In England conditions are similar, if less spectacular. And reflecting English school life are numerous novels. At the head of the list are E. F. Benson's *David Blaize,* and Compton Mackenzie's *Sinister Street,* and the stories of Winchester life, *Sonia* and *Christopher.* There is the more proved *Stalky,* and others, as many, to adapt Catullus, as the sands on the shore or the stars in the heavens.

Of all these *Tom Brown's School-Days* (its more popular title) is first, and the rest are nowhere. In boyhood you thrill at the cricket match, at hare and hounds, and at the fight between Tom Brown and Slogger Williams. And in manhood you return to these adventures and are thrilled once more. One reason for an early friendship with *Tom Brown* was his accessibility. Our parents gave us the book. They did not give us *The Red Tomahawk,* or *Forty Buckets of Blood.* We read these too, but not overtly. It was a rare sensation to enjoy a parental book, but it was a genuine one. The astounding fact was that *Tom Brown* compared favorably with *Ragged Dick.* It was almost enough to make children respect the reading taste of their parents. *Tom Brown* is still a popular book. Annually twenty-five novels of school life compete for oblivion, but *Tom Brown* is even now read by thousands of boys of all ages.

Such vogue in America seems more remarkable in the light of one distinct handicap afflicting *Tom Brown.*

The Parent of School-Boy Novels

The book is enveloped in a haze of localisms. What is a "Præpostor"? "Fagging"? What does it mean to "slipper on the hands" or to "bottle the swipes"? Mysteries, yet no boy takes the edge from the story by discovering in a dictionary that this last means transforming the ale, drunk with the hard Gloucester cheese, into a respectable drink. And the story is read with as much interest as ever. When future college youths read the school-boy novels written today, will they be as tolerant of our *argot* as we have been of Rugby slang? Will they raise a curious eyebrow over our jargon? These are academic queries, for the school novels of our day will be, as has been said, in Hades, boasting that *Tom Brown* sent them there. *Tom Brown* holds its own in spite of its vernacular.

One reason for this is clear. Doff the Rugby wrappings of Scud and Brooke: their experience of life is the experience of school-boys the world over. Tom is more real than Stalky, or Stover, or the adolescents in *This Side of Paradise*. The boy who waggles his ear to warn his fellow that the catchword for the master is "gerund," not "gerundive," merely images the genius of Tom. Other writers have shown us with some elaborateness the trappings of boyhood; somehow Hughes did more: he caught the very spirit of the unaccommodated boy, the "thing itself." A headmaster, when first shown the manuscript, said: "Let it be published. It will be the book for all future public-school boys."

Another reason for the popularity of *Tom Brown's*

School-Days is that it is more than a book for boys. Returning to it in middle life, the reader finds much that was invisible in his youth; in every episode he discerns new meanings. The book and its sequel, *Tom Brown at Oxford,* now seem didactic; Hughes is evidently preaching a nineteenth-century gospel. Just as in *Gulliver's Travels* Swift's satire may remain unperceived; as in *Tom Jones* Fielding's Homeric allusions may be ignored; so Hughes's deeper wisdom is reserved for maturer study. Hughes has something to say; a charge which cannot be preferred lightly against the authors of modern school novels. The reader realizes that *Tom Brown* must be classified anew. For it belongs to the very small group of books in English literature which appeal to a double audience. *Tom Brown's School-Days* has a twofold appeal: to school-boys and to students of Victorian thought.

One extraordinary mood of this book is the delight in physical exercise. The style of football played at Rugby seems paleolithic, but it had the vigour which prompted Wellington's *mot* on the relation of the fields of Eton and Rugby to that of Waterloo. Tom's triumphs on the football field were prior to the time of interscholastic matches. Rugby customs and Rugby football were laws unto themselves. "Winchester," sing the Eton boys, "we know; Harrow we know; but who the hell are you?" Rugby was savage in the early days, and this fact the others have not quite forgotten. Nevertheless, from one phase of the Rugby game of football was born the

American college game, although, thanks to an army of experts, the child has now changed amazingly.

"This stone," so reads the tablet at Rugby, "commemorates the exploit of William Webb Ellis, who with a fine disregard of the rules of football as played in his time first took the ball in his arms and ran with it thus originating the distinctive feature of the Rugby game."

Hughes delighted in the ferocity of these contests. His interest in them was fervid, almost religious. Now this zeal for muscle was no wayward enthusiasm of the author's; it was almost a dogma in one trend of Victorian thought. For Hughes was a Christian Socialist, and one tenet in his creed was the utmost in bodily vigour. Kingsley preached lustiness and damned lassitude till it seemed a disgrace not to feel like an athlete at the crest of his training. Lancelot Smith in *Yeast* and Amyas Leigh in *Westward Ho!* denounce asceticism and laud athleticism till the irritated reader is certain that there can be no truth in either doctrine. So in *Tom Brown's School-Days* Hughes pictures the ideal English boyhood, a novitiate in muscular Christianity.

The doctrine is rather violently illustrated by Tom's battle with Slogger Williams. This is a battle reminiscent of Hughes's own days at Rugby. Years afterward an ecclesiastic rose at a dinner party and called out to Mr. J. G. Holliday, one of the seconds in this fight, now a lawyer: "Why, it's Buz!'" It was Slogger Williams. Whereupon the two shook hands and then fought this fight again, outlying the veterans of all wars; they fought it busily, absorbedly, down Ludgate Hill and Fleet Street, down the Strand to the Law Courts. It might be an exaggeration to say that Hughes believed in fighting. Yet he had no marked distaste for a brutal, if fair, encounter. In fact, his conclusion in *Tom Brown* is not unlike Shakespeare's "Beware of entrance to a quarrel, but being in. . . ." Here once more Hughes is echoing Kingsley and the red-corpuscled socialists; for he says: "And if you do fight, fight it out, and don't give in while you can stand and see."

Such two-fisted manliness should be, Hughes thought, the answer of every English boy to bullying, or of every Englishman throughout life. Physical bullying in school, intellectual bullying in Victorian England—to both the answer is to be the same: uncompromising manly resistance. The Victorian age was an age of bullying, of the imposition of opinions, according to Kingsley. In the preface to the sixth edition of *Tom Brown,* Hughes inveighs against this evil. His remedy is by such intrinsic manliness in youth to check the bullying of later life. What dreams in the 'sixties could compare with those of the Christian Socialists?

In *Tom Brown at Oxford* Hughes alludes frequently to more subtle movements of thought of the epoch. No one could be at Oxford in the 'fifties and remain unaware of the complex ethics of the Anglo-Catholics, or be unmindful of the voices of Carlyle, Mill, and Tennyson. But in *Tom Brown's School-Days* the focus is upon the simple doctrines of the

Christian Socialists, applied to boyhood. Introspection hardly exists; there is little theology. Hughes was basically unaffected by the Oxford Movement. The ideas with which he, Maurice, and Kingsley are concerned are almost naïve: physical welfare, manliness, tenderness for the weak, and direct appeal to God for the solution of daily problems. These, the Christian Socialist leaders believed, satisfied the needs of the average man; their spirit is stamped upon every page of *Tom Brown's School-Days*.

And the thought of the Broad Churchmen and the Christian Socialists is most real in this book, not through episodes but through characters. Translated, some of them are the real protagonists in the drama of the Broad Church Movement acted in England in the 'fifties and 'sixties. Arthur, in spite of assertions that he was Arthur Walrond, will always represent for many readers Arthur Penhryn Stanley. Brooke is presumably George Hughes, the brother of the author, and stroke of the 1843 Oxford crew which defeated Cambridge with seven oars. East has been identified as William Patrick Adam, later governor of Madras.

One character, the greatest, is shown undisguised. In *Tom Brown's School-Days* occurs the most natural picture of the man who succeeded, as the saying was, in changing the face of education throughout England—Thomas Arnold. Even in Dean Stanley's biography there is nothing more personally winning than Hughes's sketches of Dr. Arnold in the study with Tom, or preaching the school sermon. In

Hughes's reverent account of him as he talked to the boys of "Jesus Christ, the Man," he seems an embodiment of the ideals of Christian Socialism. One thinks of his son's tribute in *Rugby Chapel:* "O strong soul, by what shore tarriest thou now?"

What of Tom? Hughes denies that he has a prototype, but students of the movement of Christian Socialism will always think of him as Kingsley or as Hughes. The resemblances between Tom Brown and Tom Hughes are striking: at Rugby their athletic eminence, their stalwart open-mindedness, their faith in a personal Christ; at Oxford their indifference to the Anglo-Catholic Movement, and their rescues from wandering fires by the love of good women. Hughes's later life is the kind one would predict for Tom Brown. A student of law, the chaplain of Lincoln's Inn, the president of a workingman's college, the founder of co-operative societies and of a Christian Socialist community in America, Hughes was, much more than Kingsley, another incarnation of the ideals of the Christian Socialists. Hughes is Tom Brown grown up. The virile boy has become the great, strapping Berkshireman whom Lowell loved.

Such glimpses *Tom Brown's School-Days* gives into the thought of the Victorians. But after all the first message of the book is the more significant—the message to young men in school and college. When Hughes wrote *Tom Brown* he gave his best, and though there are *The Manliness of Christ* and other volumes, Hughes is known now for *Tom*

Brown. Literary form was sacrificed to what Hughes had to say. The book is without artistry of any kind. It is, indeed, if one is hostile, a "preachy" book. But the advice that Hughes gives is profound, and is apposite today. Pick up at a bookstore the yarns of school and college, the volumes of vapid counsel on school life; you may return thoughtfully to the advice Tom's father gave him as he placed him on the coach for Rugby, or to the lessons which Tom learned at first hand from his fellows and from the greatest of schoolmasters, Thomas Arnold. Moreover, Tom Brown is not merely the best, it is the first school-boy book. Nothing of this sort had ever been written save Lamb's account of *Christ's Hospital* or Dickens's tales of Squeers's school in *Nicholas Nickleby*. Hughes was the pioneer. *Tom Brown* ran through five editions in nine months. A copy, it is said, is still given to every boy at Rugby. It is the parent of all school-boy novels.

INDEX

Index

popularity of, 89; *Good Shepherd with the Kid,* 158; *Heinrich Heine* (quoted), 125; *Immortality,* 152; *Irish Essays,* 158; *Joubert* (quoted), 144; *Letters;* sources of Arnold's opinions of his contemporaries, 100–107; Quoted: 100, 101, 102, 104, 105, 106, 107, 135, 142; Mentioned: 98, 127, 136, 158; *Literature and Dogma;* editions of, 88, 89; Mentioned: 85, 91; *The Literary Influence of Academies* (quoted), 125; *Marcus Aurelius,* 154; *Maurice de Guérin* (quoted), 143, 153, 158; *Merope;* editions of, 89; preface to (quoted), 132; illustration of Arnold's poetic theories, 141–142; its failure, 142; Mentioned: 91, 102, 127, 154, 155; *Mixed Essays;* poetic theories in, 127; *Modern Element in Literature* (quoted), 154; *Morality,* 151; *Mycerinus;* criticism of, 79; emphasis on philosophical ideas, 116–118; plot, 116–118; character of Mycerinus, 116–118; failure to satisfy Arnold's ideals, 133–134; Quoted: 75, 117, 118; Mentioned: 85, 152; *Narrative Poems;* editions of, 89; *New Poems* (1867); Swinburne's review of, 83, 103; editions of, 88; Mentioned, 77; *New Sirens;* criticism of in *Fraser's,* 78; Swinburne's connection with, 99, 103–104, 158; *Notebooks,* 154; *Obermann,* 151, 156; *On Translating Homer;* first attack on complacency, 80; editions of, 89, 154; *Pagan and Mediaeval Religious Sentiment,* 154; *Philomela,* 159, 160; *Poems by A.;* published, 1849, 73; reviewed by London *Times,* 75; by *Fraser's,* 78; *Poems of 1853,* 77; *Poems of 1855,* 77; *Preface of 1853;* as expression of Arnold's poetic theories, 127; acknowledgment of weakness of *Empedocles,* 127; treatment of Aristotelian themes in, 129; first formulation of his poetic theories, 132; Quoted: 130; Mentioned: 126, 133, 134, 136, 137, 141, 160; *Preface of 1854;* as expression of Arnold's poetic theories, 127; Quoted: 126; Mentioned: 133, 134, 136, 141, 160; *Rachel,* 158; *Rugby Chapel,* 159; (quoted), 282; *St. Paul and Protestantism;* editions of, 88, 89; *Scholar-Gipsy;* editions of, 89; influence of, 92; Mentioned: 134, 151, 159, 237; *Selected Poems;* editions of, 86, 88, 89; *Self-Dependence;* editions of, 90, 151; *The Sick King in Bokhara;* emphasis on philosophical ideas, 116; plot, 119–120; its failure to satisfy Arnold's ideals, 133–134; *Sohrab and Rustum;* criticism of in *Fraser's,* 78; popularity of, 83, 89, 90; illustration of Arnold's theories, 133, 134–141, 142, 149; Arnold's opinion of, 135; source of, 136; weakness of, 137–140; Quoted: 138, 139; Mentioned: 102, 116, 120, 150; *The Strayed Reveller, and Other Poems;* illustration of Arnold's Hellenism, 120–122; connection with Milton's *Comus,* 120–121; Quoted: 121, 150; Mentioned: 77, 92, 155, 159; *The Study of Poetry,* 145; *A Summer Night,* 150, 169; *Sweetness and Light;* editions

Index

compared with *Sohrab and Rustum,* 136; Newman on, 230–231; Mentioned: 178.

Calvin, John, 19; influence upon Henry Gosse, 63.

Carlyle, Thomas, His *Life of John Sterling* a picture of the age, 3–7; his importance in, 14–15; connection with Sterling, 3–10, 12–17; portraits of his contemporaries (quoted), 6–7; appearance in Sterling's *Onyx Ring,* 8; as critic of literature, 8, 14; criticisms of Sterling's work, 8–9; portraits of Coleridge, 9–10, 11; in old age (quoted), 11; problem of his religious views, 12–14; Emerson's description of, 15; Sterling's summary of their friendship, 17; importance of his *Past and Present,* 21–22, 24–25, 39–42; value of his suggested reforms, 22–24; his artistic methods in *Past and Present,* 25–29; structure of, 29–30; attacks on English apathy, 28–29; use of *Chronica Jocelini,* 30–34; problems of government, religion, and leadership, 34–37; faults in his theories, 37–39; Henry James on, 39; Ruskin on, 40; criticism of Kingsley's *Alton Locke* (quoted), 45; influence on Kingsley, 55, 171; his opinion of Newman, 62; attacks on Philistinism by means of "Bobus Higgins," 80; Arnold's opinions of, 106; reflection of social unrest in writings of, 163, 164, 165, 166; opinion of Elliott, 178; Elliott's regard for, 180; opinion of Cooper's *Purgatory of Suicides* (quoted), 181; Brimley's essay on his *Life of John Sterling,* 205; on Tennyson, 209; Clough's opinion of, 241; influence upon Clough, 247–248; descriptions of Landor (quoted), 266–267, 268; Quoted: 4, 8–9, 11, 14, 21, 25, 40, 41, 42, 59, 79, 130, 163, 275; Mentioned: 47, 51, 52, 170, 176, 180, 201, 251, 280; Works: *The French Revolution;* Carlyle's opinion of (quoted), 25; influence upon *Alton Locke,* 55; Landor's opinion of, 268; Mentioned: 5, 26; *Life of John Sterling;* accurate picture of the age, 3–7; serenity of tone in, 4, 5; power of, 6; portrait of Coleridge in, 10, 11; evidences of Carlyle's religious views in, 14; Carlyle's opinion of (quoted), 14; medium for Carlyle's opinions, 14; its most extraordinary aspect, 15; Brimley's essay on, 205; Quoted: 7, 15; *Past and Present;* value of, 21–22, 24–25, 39–42; Morley's opinion of, 24; Carlyle's artistic methods in, 25–27; his grotesques, 27–28; effectiveness of, 28–29; structure, 29–30; illustrations of his theories in, 30–37; his opinion of (quoted), 39; influence upon Kingsley's *Yeast,* 55; attacks on Philistinism in, 80; reflection of social unrest in, 163; *Proem,* outlines Carlyle's purpose in *Past and Present,* 29; *The Ancient Monk* (second book of *Past and Present*), 22, 29, 30; source, 30; Carlyle's use of, 30–34; study in hero-worship, 37; characters of,

Index

"Coleridge Moonshine," Intellectual fashion, 10; effect upon Sterling and others, 12.

Colvin, Sidney, On Landor, 255.

Comte, Auguste, Brimley's opinion of, 205–206; Mentioned: 201.

Cook, Edward *Literary Recreations* (quoted), 73.

Cook, Eliza, 167, 181.

Cooper, Thomas, His *Autobiography of a Chartist*, 54; interest in social conditions, 167; his *Purgatory of Suicides*, 180; Carlyle's opinion of, 181; his poetry, 180–181; *Chartist Hymn* (quoted), 181; Mentioned: 182.

Cowper, William, Newman on, 224–225.

Crabbe, George, Newman's interest in, 232; Clough's opinion of, 241; *Tales of the Hall;* Newman on, 232; Mentioned: 167, 177.

Dante Alighieri, Arnold on, 103, 108, 132, 148, 155; master of Rossetti, 192; Landor's opinion of, 261, 268.

Darwin, Charles, 13, 30, 60.

De Quincey, Thomas, Praise of Landor's *Gebir*, 263; Mentioned: 10.

Dickens, Charles, Called Schnüspel in Carlyle's *Past and Present*, 27; Brimley's opinion of, 205; Works: *Bleak House;* Landor's resemblance to Boythorn, 255, 266; *Nicholas Nickleby;* Squeers' school in, 283; Mentioned: 48, 181, 201.

Disraeli, Benjamin (Earl of Beaconsfield), Opinion of Arnold (quoted), 81; Arnold on, 101, footnote; Mentioned: 38, 181.

Dobson, Austin, 85.

Dryden, John, Arnold on, 97, 148; praised by Newman, 224; Mentioned: 127, 178.

Edgeworth, Frank, Carlyle's description of, 6, 7.

Eliot, George, Opinion of Arnold's poetry, 93; Newman's dislike of, 230; Mentioned: 49, 166.

Elliott, Ebenezer, Poet of social reform, 166–167, 176–180; violence of his poetry, 176–178; effect upon his contemporaries, 178; theories of poetry, 179–180; Works: *Corn Law Rhymes,* 54, 178; *The Exile,* 177; *The Jacobin's Prayer* (quoted), 178; *The Letter,* 177; *The Ranter,* 177; *The Splendid Village,* 177; *The Village Patriarch,* 177; Quoted: 176, 177, 178, 179, 180; Mentioned: 54, 170, 182.

Emerson, Ralph Waldo, Sterling's *Strafford* dedicated to, 8; anecdote of Coleridge (quoted), 10; on Carlyle (quoted), 15, 22; friendship with Sterling, 15, 16; letters of Sterling to, 16, 17; connection with Arnold, 97, 106; Clough's estimate of, 241; Mentioned: 247, 271.

Index

Index

Index

Robinson, Henry Crabb, *Diary;* Arnold on, 104; account of Landor's criticisms (quoted), 261.

Rossetti, Christina, On her brother (quoted), 197.

Rossetti, Dante Gabriel, Social unrest of age reflected in poetry of, 163; popularity of, 185–187; modern criticism of, 187–188; aestheticism, 188–190; *Blessed Damozel,* and *Jenny* as interpretations of, 189–198; conception of womanhood, 197–198; Quoted: 55, 82, 192, 196, 198; Mentioned: 108, 262; Works: *The Blessed Damozel;* popularity of, 185–187; as interpretation of Rossetti, 190–194; origin of, 191–192; resemblances between her and Jenny, 196–198; *Dante at Verona,* 192; *Day-dream,* 191; *Ecce Ancilla Domini,* 191; *The House of Life;* influence of, 186; *Jenny,* as interpretation of Rossetti, 190, 195–198; Swinburne's criticism of, 195–196; Mentioned: 163; *Mary's Girlhood,* 191; *The Portrait,* 187; *The Stream's Secret,* 186, 191; *Venus Verticordia,* 191.

Rossetti, William Michael, 15.

Ruskin, John, Estimate of Carlyle (quoted), 40; Arnold's opinion of, 106; his *Modern Painters,* 35, 59, 165; Mentioned: 29, 35, 57, 59, 165.

Ryder, Ignatius Dudley, Account of Newman, 216, 225; Quoted: 216, 227, 228–229, 230.

Saintsbury, George, Criticism of Arnold's theories, 132; on Arnold, 159; on Hood, 175; Mentioned: 203.

Salisbury, Robert Gascoigne-Cecil (Lord), Arnold on, 101, footnote.

Saturday Review, On Arnold (quoted), 82; Mentioned: 81.

"School-Boy Novels," 275–277.

Scott, Sir Walter, Influence of his novels, 31–32; his influence upon Newman, 225–228; Newman's tributes to, 226, 227; Mentioned: 10, 210, 228; Works: *Bride of Lammermoor,* 226; *Guy Mannering,* 226; *Ivanhoe,* 227; *Lay of the Last Minstrel,* 226; *Marmion;* Landor's opinion of, 261; *Quentin Durward,* 227; *Waverly,* 226.

Shakespeare, William, Carlyle's opinion of, 8; Arnold's criticism of, 144; Newman's familiarity with, 219; Mentioned: 68, 97, 99, 103, 132, 135, 137, 148, 152, 185, 271; *Hamlet,* 185, 271; *King Lear,* 136; *Macbeth,* 130, 133, 136, 137; *Othello;* Brimley on, 207–208, 271.

Shelley, Percy Bysshe, Arnold's opinions of, 97, 105, 144; compared with Brimley's, 210–211; Brimley's opinion of, 108; (quoted), 211–212; connection with Landor, 259, 262–263, 264; *Prometheus Unbound,* 263; Mentioned: 73, 74, 91, 107, 260.

Sheridan, Richard Brinsley, 48, 185.

296

Index